DARK
PSYCHOLOGY

How to Master the Art of Dark Persuasion and
Covert Manipulation

(Practice Mind Hacking With Manipulation
Techniques)

Lorraine Boone

Published by Sharon Lohan

© **Lorraine Boone**

All Rights Reserved

Dark Psychology: How to Master the Art of Dark Persuasion and Covert Manipulation (Practice Mind Hacking With Manipulation Techniques)

ISBN 978-1-990334-58-0

Legal & Disclaimer

The information contained in this book is not designed to replace or take the place of any form of medicine or professional medical advice. The information in this book has been provided for educational and entertainment purposes only.

The information contained in this book has been compiled from sources deemed reliable, and it is accurate to the best of the Author's knowledge; however, the Author cannot guarantee its accuracy and validity and cannot be held liable for any errors or omissions. Changes are periodically made to this book. You must consult your doctor or get professional medical advice before using any of the suggested remedies, techniques, or information in this book.

Upon using the information contained in this book, you agree to hold harmless the Author from and against any damages, costs, and expenses, including any legal fees potentially resulting from the application of any of the information provided by this guide. This disclaimer applies to any damages or injury caused by the use and application, whether directly or indirectly, of any advice or information presented, whether for breach of contract, tort, negligence, personal injury, criminal intent, or under any other cause of action.

You agree to accept all risks of using the information presented inside this book. You need to consult a professional medical practitioner in order to ensure you are both able and healthy enough to participate in this program.

Table of Contents

Introduction

You wake up at four in the morning on your day off. You're panting, sweating, and are inexplicably anxious. You can't remember having a dream. You can't recall eating or drinking anything before going to bed to induce such a horrible waking experience.

So, what's wrong with you?

Perhaps it's something much darker than you realize. Perhaps someone has targeted you and you've been completely unaware of it.

Does someone want what you have?

As humans, we've learned to accumulate certain things and people to make our lives as easy as possible. We find a mate to share our lives with and the responsibilities that come along with our lives. We find a job to pay for all the things we're going to not only need but want. We buy a home to raise our family in. We buy the things we need, like automobiles to transport our families and us to where we need to go.

So far, we've got a pretty good list of things people feel that they need: a mate – a job – a home – a car. And we're willing to work for these things. But not everyone is willing to work the way we are.

Some people wish to take the lazy way in life. They would rather let someone else accumulate these things, then they will edge in, push you out of the way and take over everything you worked so hard for.

Don't fool yourself into thinking this idea is far-fetched and not worth worrying about. Think about how many divorces there are. Think about how many times you've found someone eyeing your mate, your job, your home, your car. Now, think about the stories you've heard of people going missing. Someone has to take over what they left behind, right?

Someone has to come into the distraught mate's life who was left all alone. Someone has to take over the job they left vacant. Someone has to move into the home to take the place left by the vacant mate. And someone has to drive the car they left too. Many believe that it might as well be them. And some would prefer not to wait for someone to pass on from natural causes before they take over what will be left behind.

Insidious, you say?

I agree it is. And it happens all the time.

Not everyone will kill to replace someone. Many merely use mental techniques to acquire what they desire. They learn how to get into other people's heads to make them do what they want them to.

They can get into your head, the head of your boss, and even the head of your mate. They can warp things to bend in their favor while making you seem inadequate in ways you had no idea you were. They might even make you feel as if you should let them have what you've worked for – as if they're better equipped to deal with things than you are.

Even the most secure individuals can be made to feel insecure. They can be made to feel as if they're not entirely sane and not seeing things the right way. Once you think that maybe you're wrong about something, you've already given someone else the upper hand.

Not that you should always think you're right about every little thing. No one is right about everything. But beware of that person who is telling you that you are not what you think you are. Beware of the person who doles out backhanded compliments to you. Beware of that person who tells you often how lucky you are to have what you do.

Luck has nothing to do with what you've gotten for yourself and your life. Hard work, perseverance, and using your brain has gotten you where you are today. Luck had little to nothing to do with it.

In this book, I'll let you in on some secrets that you can keep a lookout for. There's no reason for you to wake up in a panicked state again. If some dark individual comes snooping around you and what you've made of your life, you will recognize them quickly and get rid of them. You will defend that life you built against anyone who threatens it. And you will do so, using the same techniques the darkness wanted to use against you.

It's time to learn how to get into the minds of what some consider monsters. I hope you're ready.

Chapter 1: Dark Psychology: Meaning

The study of psychology has had an indubitable effect on human self-awareness and understanding of emotions, but the topic reaches far further than that and has a much greater influence on our day to day lives than many give it credit for. Psychology in plain terms is defined as the study of the science behind the thoughts, emotions and behaviors that govern each human based on their personal history or inclination toward learned or developed behaviors. In other words, people who pursue an interest in psychology are inspired by curiosity and a thirst for knowledge of why people are the way that they are. Dark Psychology carries that query into the hidden sections of the human consciousness, the aspects that people try to neglect, to bury or to cover up (if they are even aware of them).

Others use their hidden knowledge of dark psychological techniques to manipulate the thoughts of others, achieve dominance over others or influence people's actions, with their victims sometimes never suspecting that their thoughts or deeds have been compromised. Some of the most commonly read and talked about sub-sections of Dark Psychology include:

I. Cyberstalking and Virtual Predatory Behavior: This subset includes personalities as mild as internet bullies on social media platforms to the most severe like virtual identity thieves.

II. Political Psychology: This falls into the category of Dark Psychology, depending on the subject of study.

III. Behavioral Psychology: Individuals spend a fair amount of time studying the traits of Dark Psychology and how they can influence the behavior of other individuals.

There are several Dark Psychology techniques in practice, and people have used the art of self-promotion to boost their careers. Those who have made indelible marks in the entertainment industry and those who dominate many artistic professions have thanked psychological tactics of persuasion and reading people for their progress within their chosen fields. Each individual's experience with Dark Psychology in their lifetime certainly depends on their character, and whether their aim is to prevent themselves from being a target of dark psychological tactics or if they prefer to use them on others as a way of advancing their position, benefiting from a certain situation or knowingly causing harm.

HISTORY OF DARK PSYCHOLOGY AND ITS IMPACT ON THE MODERN WORLD

If Dark Psychology is such a matter of concern, why is it still considered such a newly established part of the psychological field? Some of the key reasons for this is that while psychology overall is still a recent phenomenon in medical literature, Dark Psychology as an area of research is one of the latest innovations in psychology since it has been recognized as a significant topic in modern culture. Dark Psychology made a big impact on the field in the early 2000s as psychologists around the world were motivated and inspired to better understand cybercriminals, starting to collect information that had been gathered about criminal psychology and analyzing individuals to either capture them or anticipate their next exploits before they ever had an opportunity to set them off. Study into the personality traits associated with Dark Psychology (also known as malevolence characteristics) has been underway for decades, contributing to some of the world's biggest advances in justice and criminal law, such as:

I. Criminal profiling and investigative branches of service devoted to research and development from county-level police to foreign enforcement teams at government levels.

II. Introduction of new regulations to protect us from the most evil among us who would not have been punished by law before.

III. Stretching prison sentences for the most malevolent, or delivering psychiatric and social treatment for their disorders that were not acknowledged by medical and legal institutions in the years before a particular case.

Currently, Dark Psychology is well considered to be of special concern to those examining the minds, emotions and behavior of offenders operating within the cyber world for tactical gain and worldwide advantage. Across the entertainment industry, there have been numerous applications made for it which continue to be investigated, including high-quality insightful shows on true crime cases and fictitious criminals and crime solvers with profound and humanizing qualities, that have drawn people's interest at all political, academic, social and class levels all over the globe[BA1]. More than anything, Dark Psychology and its increasing prominence have caused all those who are unwilling to accept the darker aspects of human nature to rise and take note, acknowledging the fact that even the happiest and most positive of people may be characterized by darker traits. Each individual is made up of both positive and negative attributes, habits and behaviors that are influenced or created by events that they have experienced and the people who surround them. It is perfectly natural for each person to have questions about their personality, feelings, emotions and behavior that can be answered by the research and studies undertaken in Dark Psychology.

HOW DARK PSYCHOLOGY AFFECTS HUMANS

There are nine personality traits that researchers usually associate with people who are of interest to Dark Psychology analysis. Sometimes recognized as the "Traits of Malevolence" these character indicators shape the basis of darker personalities, and knowing them will help to identify their use around you, whether deliberate or otherwise.

TWO CAN MAKE A PATTERN

Displaying only one of the recognizable characteristics is not enough for anyone to be firmly branded a dark personality. If they only fall within one group of indicators, then it might only be a chance of experiencing a childhood trauma or a challenging series of conditions that they encounter that proves to have a huge impact on the development of that individual's personality. In situations such as these where the trait is dangerous to the person or others, or where the person is unable to recognize this aspect of himself or herself and creates certain psychological problems, the person may seek the help of a counselor or other psychological health provider to recognize their issues and to figure out how best to handle them in the future.

Here is a closer look at the dark traits shown and established in individuals who are guided by their Dark Psychology.

I. Narcissism: Narcissists are people whose behavior, feelings and interests center around their own well-being and success above others, and often to the detriment of others. This personality feature is influenced by the Greek myth of Narcissus, a man who spent his life in love with his own image. Narcissists tend not to operate well in organizations and can instantly be outraged if others seek to supervise them.

II. Excessively Reactive Egos: Often widely referred to as Egotists, individuals with overly sensitive egos may appear like narcissists on paper, but there is a crucial distinction between them. Like narcissists, individuals with overly sensitive egos are concerned about their own development and success in life, but unlike narcissists who have an inherently high view about themselves, egotists and others who exhibit this tendency evaluate their self-worth based on what others think about them. When others praise them, their self-worth improves, and they can perform without paying too much attention to their environment, whether at work or at home. It is when egotists and others with excessively sensitive egos are rebuked or questioned that their deeper side shows, and it can show itself in several ways, such as complacency or anti-social behaviors.

III. Elevated Self-Interest: Individuals with elevated self-interest are also centered on their own advancement and well-being, to the extent of fleeing or leaving others. This attribute is often associated with remarkable personal ambition and motivation that enables them to stand out among their colleagues. Sadly, like narcissists and egotists, they may not perform well in team or community settings but seem to succeed in leadership positions and having control over others as long as they have somebody to answer to that has a more moderate or positive temperament and behavioral style.

IV. Personal Entitlement: These are individuals who believe that everything on this planet should belong to them. While the nuances differ from person to person, entitled individuals feel they deserve what they see others getting. It could be trivial, like belongings or the sum of money that someone else makes. It could be broader than that, believing that they deserve love and affection without needing to earn it or find it as most people do. Their darkest traits emerge when they have been refused something to which they believe they are entitled. One of the most prominent instances of moral privilege used in trait analysis is that of spoiled children. Entitlement is an acquired characteristic that many individuals grow out of in their adolescent years or into adulthood, but it can be prompted or triggered by factors such as financial status, social class and personal success (or loss, based on individual circumstances).

V. Manipulative Tendency: People living on the dark side of psychology are considered to have a talent for deceit. This may be as subtle as using a talent for deception to ensure that they have the best sales figures each week, to those who use their talents for political gain, or find themselves influencing others through mind control and other destructive tactics.

Sometimes referred to as the "Machiavellian characteristic," those who display expertise for the strategic coercion of others for their benefit are named after the political scientist Niccolò Machiavelli. Machiavelli's political views were centered on the principle that the means used to accomplish a certain objective are often worth it in the end (often irrespective of the cost or harm caused, as long as the manipulator is not adversely affected).

VI. Moral Disengagement: This is the term widely used to characterize people who truly believe that any laws in effect do not apply to them. Those who have this behavioral trait are considered to believe that they are above the law and are thus free to to take action that others would find immoral or unethical without having any sort of moral obligation, remorse or embarrassment after the act.

VII. Psychopathy and Psychopathic Tendencies: An individual who has been labeled a "psychopath" has been described by qualified psychologists or personality specialists as having a personality disorder called Psychopathy, in which a person lacks sympathy or compassion for anyone or anything. The term "psychopath" has invaded the mainstream vocabulary as a well-known generic term for serial killers and other delinquents that fall into that type of character. They have become popular in TV series and horror movies, but this remains one of the most misconstrued characteristics that is still being explored and researched because more and more is being discovered about the psychopathic mind.

VIII. Sadism and Sadistic Behaviors: A sadist is someone who has been described as displaying sadistic behavioral patterns or, as part of their developed personality, having a propensity towards inflicting suffering or embarrassment to others (and getting gratification from these misdeeds) as a way of expressing their dominance and control over others. The harm does not always have to be physical or psychological. This personality trait is often related to sexual dominance as well as to the demonstration of emotional and psychological control.

IX. Spitefulness and Malicious Predispositions: Malice is the intention and ability to inflict harm or to cause damage and also the readiness to take such action even if it means injuring oneself in the process (physically, mentally or psychologically). These malicious features can appear in any variety of human behaviors but should be taken very seriously when they are identified, and treated with the utmost caution, as the risk of personal damage by association is elevated with those who have daily interactions with malicious individuals.

THE DARK TRIAD AND THEIR ROLES IN DARK PSYCHOLOGY

While all of the characteristics described above can be seen in individuals with dark personality traits, there are three key attributes that some psychologists say must be present for anyone to be considered a focus for Dark Psychology. Manipulation, Psychopathy and Narcissism are the core components of what is known in psychological contexts as the Dark Triad. The Dark Triad is the basis for most of the Dark Psychology studies, as these traits are the three most prominent attributes exhibited by those who are researched within the field of Dark Psychology.

Throughout this article, we will take a more thorough look at how these traits can be clearly expressed in various forms of behavior, how to recognize their strategies, and how to protect yourself from them. Continue reading to know more about the dark side of human psychology and how it works just about anywhere you look, from famous marketing campaigns to people on the street!

Chapter 2: Who Uses Dark Psychology?

Many people will use dark psychology to their advantage. We often think this is something we will see on an occasional basis, not something that is so prevalent or so important. And we like to be proud of being able to stay as far away as possible because we think we will be able to recognize it long before it undergoes our lives.

Following the ideas we talked about in the previous chapter, it is safe to say that anyone can work with dark psychology to get what they want from other people. It could be anyone out there, as long as they are okay, causing some kind of damage to the target to get what they want or achieve their goals.

Most of us will assume that we will never feel comfortable causing harm to those around us. We fear that we will be expelled from society and that we would end up in prison or something else would happen to us. Often, the worry of feeling remorse and guilt in the process will be enough to keep most people away from the use of dark psychology and some of the other techniques we will talk about in this guide.

We all still have a level of dark psychology found in us. Some will keep it a little louder than others. Some of us will go all our lives and will be able to reject any impulse we have when it comes to these thoughts and actions that we may feel like doing. Laws, our ethics, and more will prevent us from working on this, and we will endure them and not harm others.

Then, some of those who will have these impulses and, for the most part, can keep them under control. They don't always go in search of targets in the hope of causing some trouble for another person along the way. But there may be a time when they cause some harm to another person, or perhaps they see another person being harmed and feel no remorse at all. Maybe they feel a little happy and happy about this in the process, especially if that fact has allowed them to get what they want. They can still suppress these dark impulses for the most part.

And then there will be those people who are unable to suppress these dark impulses, or have no desire or cure to try to delete them. They might think that others are stupid for not trying to take full advantage of them to get what they want. They have no problem using other people and other things as long as they help them get what they want.

Often, pursuing them to get what they want is harming another person. This may not be the ultimate goal of these manipulators. They could try their best to achieve their goal. If someone can be used and is not harmed in the process, then that's fine. However, if someone has to hurt themselves to achieve their goals, the dark manipulator won't feel bad either. This means that they do not necessarily have to cause harm to another person in the process intentionally, but if someone is harmed, then they are.

And you will find that many people will fall into these categories and that doesn't necessarily mean they do one type of business for one job or another. They can come from any kind of social or economic experience and have many friends or no friends. There is not necessarily a group of people who are more likely to bend in one direction or another, which can make it difficult to pinpoint who will be in dark psychology and who will be able to hide some of the impulses they have.

That said, this is good news for you. It means that you will be able to use dark psychology no matter what background you have or where you come from. Some of the best shadowy manipulators out there are those who didn't expect to become this or those who at least others didn't assume to be. This allows them to join the group they want and talk to the goals they want, without adding any suspicion to the mix.

Dark psychology is something found in each of us, but most of us will be too scared to let it out and see where it can lead us. And that's a shame. Only because of some ethical background and more, we end up losing what we would like to be able to achieve in life and where we would like to be.

This does not mean that we have to go out and cause as much harm and pain to others as possible, it is the idea that sometimes taking care of yourself and your goals are the most important thing, rather than worrying about the social norms and intentions of others people. Being able to determine when each situation is the most justified will be crucial here. And this guide will show you some of the different methods you can use with each dark psychology technique so that you can be ready to use it when you are right.

Now that we've spent some time talking about how we could all use dark psychology at one point or another to help us achieve the desired results and achieve our goals, it's time to take a look at some groups, of people who are more likely to use these techniques and have no problem bringing some dark psychology to their interactions with other people.

However, you may be surprised at how many people in your life will use dark psychology to their advantage and may have already worked through you to make it happen to their position. Some of the people in your life who could use dark psychology will include:

1. Narcissists: Those who meet the clinical diagnosis of being narcissists will have their self-esteem inflated. They need to have others around to validate their belief that they are superior. They dream that others will adore and adore them and if they have to use manipulation, dark psychology and immoral persuasion, and more, they will.

2. Sociopaths: truly sociopathic people will be intelligent and charming, but also impulsive. Due to the lack of emotionality and the ability to feel remorse, these sociopaths will use some shady tactics to add a fake relationship and, therefore, benefit the other person.

3. Lawyers: Some lawyers will focus so much on trying to win the case, that they will highlight some obscure persuasion and other tactics to ensure that they can get the desired result.

4. Politicians: there are many times when a politician will use these tactics and convince others that they are right and help them get votes.

5. Sellers: Many sellers will not be as ethical as they should and will try to get that sale with the

help of some shady tactics. They will do this to motivate and convince the other person, their customers, to buy a product, even if they can track their customers.

6. Leaders: Some leaders will use these shady tactics to achieve compliance, more significant effort, or higher performance from the people below them.

7. Public Speakers: Some speakers will be happy to use these shady tactics to increase the audience's emotional state, knowing that this leads to the sale of multiple products in the back of the room and that they can get what the audience wants to train.

8. Anyone who is truly selfish. This can be anyone who has a list of himself before others. They will use the tactic to satisfy their needs first, even at someone else's expense. They don't care if anyone else is injured in the process.

As you can see, many different people can benefit from it when it comes to using dark psychology and who will use it regularly. While there are a lot of different times when you will use manipulation and persuasion and more safely and healthily to get what we want, shady tactics will ensure that the person receives it regardless of it, even if someone else is harmed. Now let's take a look at some of the different things you need to know to use dark psychology to help you see the benefits you desire.

Chapter 3: How To Defend Yourself From Dark Psychology

We are indeed human at the end of the day. It is because of this very reason that we get to dwell allot on the opinion of others in everything that we do. We always desire and adore getting validation from others so that we can subconsciously decide whether or not we shall be depressed.in this age of the millennial, the norm has become to just brag about their wealth on social media. A lot of these bragging are often than not the truth. This ultimately leads to one having a loose relationship with reality. Self-deception of this type can dig deep into the human spicy, that a victim of these may one day wake up and realize that their perfect world is only existent within their maids. Depression will closely follow suit.

The first step to attempting to defend yourself from Dark Psychology is confronting the situation and taking the stance of breaking off any illusions you may have. You will not be able to proceed normally with your life. You have to be wary of the fact that you are in control of your own choices. Then make the conscious choice of seeing things for what they are. That deal, which seems too good to be true, could actually be just that... too good to be true. The other thing you should follow is to definitely trust your instincts.

There are times that a lie has been told to you in the most skilled way imaginable, that you will end up believing. But you can feel an imbalance on some instinctive level between what should be, what is, and then what is being projected onto you. There may be no physical signs to show that hey, something is wrong, but you feel something is wrong. The next important thing when you ask questions is to listen to the responses. This may sound somewhat unbelievable because you'll listen to the answers.

The truth is that our self-disappointment can make us choose the answers we receive. We tell ourselves that we listen, but we only pay attention to the answers we want to hear rather than to the answers we receive. You may have broken the illusions around you, but some of you are still clinging to the comfort of those illusions. The pain of confronting the situation would prevent you from listening to the real answers to your questions.

Actual listening requires a certain sense of detachment, but this time around not from reality. You have to get rid of your emotions. Your detachment from our emotions would lead you to the next step, which would logically process the new information. It can complicate situations more than they already are to act irrationally. It makes your exit strategy so much difficult to let all the emotions simmer and spring to the surface.

When you face the truth, the irrational part of you may want you to let it all go hell. Your rightly justified anger can inspire you to take steps to calm your emotions in the short term. But you may come to regret these actions in the long term. I'm not saying that you should deny your emotions; I'm not saying that you do not act on these emotions.

Act quickly

It's great that you have come to terms with the reality of things. But defense against these dark manipulative tactics entail so much more. While attempting to defend you from the claws of these manipulators, is often intense and exhilarating at first. This intensity of these emotions may cause one to slowly slide into denial. The more you delay in taking any action is usually what accelerates the onset of this denial, and when it happens, there are high chances that you might relapse and end up getting trapped in the same web. This can be avoided by taking action immediately you realize that someone is trying to manipulate you. This can present itself in the simplest of ways like when informing a close friend of some reality of the particular situation may be all that's needed so set in motion a series of events that will eventually lead to your freedom.

You should know that the fabric of illusion is made from tougher material than glass after making the choice to act. The illusion could work its way back into your heart with your emotions in high gear by using fragments of your emotions to fix it. When a liar is caught in a lie, he or she may attempt to recruit others to enforce that lie when they feel that they are no longer holding you. A deceptive partner with whom you have recently broken things off would at this point try to use the other mutual relationships in your life to change your mind. If you want to get out of this unscathed, you will need both your logic and instincts.

Although the truth of the situation is that when you discover that you've been lied to consistently, you become emotionally scarred, so the issue of leaving the situation unscathed becomes silent. Priority should be given, however, to take the route that allows you to leave this toxic situation without harming yourself further. You're all over the place emotionally. Rage, anger, hurt, and deception is the iceberg's tip. But logically, you need to think. Keep your head above the water and warn yourself.

Get help fast

When you're trapped by other people's manipulations, confusion is one of the emotions you'd experience. This helps cloud your rational thinking and leaves you feeling helpless. You might even question the reality of what you are facing at this point. It would lead to denial if you continue to entertain these doubts. You're probably going to want to conclude you've got the whole situation wrong, that you misunderstood some things and came to the wrong conclusion.

Such thinking would drive back to the manipulator's arms. Resist the urge to give in by receiving a second opinion. People go to another doctor in a health crisis to get a second opinion. This is to remove any iota of doubt about the first diagnosis that you may have and to affirm the best treatment course for you.

Similarly, getting another person's opinion can help you discern the truth of the situation and what might be your next steps. Just remember, it's better to go to someone who has proved countless times they're interested in your best. The next step is to confront the perpetrator if you have the help you need. For this, I suggest you choose the scene or location. Choose a place you know that gives you the upper hand. On your part, that would require some careful planning. If the perpetrator exists in the cyber world, especially if the person swindled you of your money, you would have to involve the police and the relevant authorities. Do some of your own investigations so as to ascertain the truth. After you face the perpetrator and take the necessary steps to get out of the situation, you must start the healing process quickly.

The scale and gravity to which you were hurt, manipulated or abused do not matter. You must be able to walk past it and wait until you can "heal" your wounds, rather than sitting on your couch and reliving the past. Time would give you enough distance from your experience, but if you learned something from this book, it would be almost never healing for emotional scars. If you don't do anything about it, an unhealthy scab could form over the wound, which would make you as vulnerable if not more than you had experienced. Speak to a counselor, attend therapy, and take an active part in facilitating the healing process, whatever you choose to do. It won't happen overnight, but you are sure that you get closer to improving every day and every step you take in therapy.

Trust your instincts

While your brain interprets signals based on facts, logic, and sometimes experience, your heart works in the opposite direction by screening information through an emotional filter. The only thing that picks up vibrations is your gut instinct, which neither the heart nor the brain can pick on. And if you can groom to the point where you recognize your inner voice and are trained to react to it, you will lower your chances of being seduced by people trying to work on you with their manipulative will. To begin with, it's hard to recognize this voice. And that's because we allowed voices of doubt, self-discrimination as well as the critics ' loud voices within and without drowning out our authentic voice over the course of our lives. Your survival depends on this voice or instinct. So, trust that when it kicks in, your brain neurons can still process things in your immediate vicinity.

Some people call it intuition, and some refer to it as instinct, especially when it comes to relationships, they are undoubtedly the same thing. You must accept that it may not always make logical sense to start trusting your instincts. If you've ever been in the middle of doing something and experienced the feeling of being watched all of a sudden, then you know what I mean. You don't have eyes at the back of your head, there's no one else with you in the room, but you get the tiny shiver running down your spine and the "sudden knowledge" you're watching.

That's what I'm talking about. The first step to connect with your instinct is to decode your mind with the voices you've let in. With meditation, you can do this. Forget the chatter of "he said, she said." Concentrate on your center. You are the voice you know. Next, be careful about your thoughts. Don't just throw away the eclectic monologs in your head. Rather go with the thoughts flow.

Why do you think of a certain person in some way? How do you feel so deeply about this person, even if you only knew each other for a few days? What's that nagging feeling about this other person that you have? You get more tuned to your intuition as you explore your thoughts and understand when your instincts kick and how to react to it. You may need to learn to take a step back to pause and think if you are the kind of person who prefers to make spur decisions at the moment. This moment in which you pause gives you the opportunity to really reflect on your decisions and evaluate them. The next part is a hard part and it couldn't be followed by many people. Unfortunately, you can't skip or navigate around this step. This part has to do with trust. You need to be open to the idea of trusting yourself and trusting others to be able to trust your instinct. Your failure to trust others would just make you paranoid, and it's not your instincts that kick when you're paranoid.

It's the fear of you. Fear tends to turn every molehill into a hill. You must let go of your fear, embrace confidence, and let that lead in your new relationships. You are better able to hear the voice inside without the roadblocks put up by fear in your mind. Finally, your priorities need to be re-evaluated. If your mind is at the forefront of money and material possessions, you may not be able to see the past. Any interaction you have with people would be interpreted as people trying to take advantage of you, and if you dwell on that frequently enough, it will soon become your reality. You know how you attract into your life what you think of. If you're constantly thinking about material wealth, you're only going to attract people who think like you. Using this as a guide, look at all your relationships with this new hindsight; the old, the new, and the perspective. Don't enter a relationship that expects to be played. Be open when you approach them, whether it's a business relationship, a romantic relationship or even a regular acquaintance. You can get the right feedback about them from your intuition. Do not step into this thinking, too, that your gut will tell you to run in the opposite direction when you meet suspect people.

Chapter 4: The Power Of Persuasion

Becoming more persuasive can help us many walks of life, from making us more efficient at our jobs or helping us attract an amazing partner to successfully debating and influencing others. The ability to persuade means we have changed someone's perception on something, which otherwise would have stayed the same. This shows just how powerful this art is. We can make people think or behave in the way we want them to - now that's magic.

Throughout history the most powerful leaders and trail blazers seemingly possessed a quality which made others believe in them and subsequently follow them. These influential people mastered the art of persuasion. They had a way of communicating which made others pay attention. Most of us have met people who have a natural sense of charm and they somehow seem to easily gain the trust of others. I believe all of us are born with this natural charisma, however due to the struggles of life we lose touch with it. In this chapter, you will learn how to get back in tune with your natural persuasive abilities.

To understand what makes people persuadable we have to learn what makes them tick first. We do this of course by looking under the hood at human psychology. Changing the way people think involves altering their attitudes, values, beliefs and goals which then impacts what action they take in the future.

Persuasion is made-up of 6 main aspects -

Intent – Persuasion should come across quite naturally but with intention. We want people to see our perspective on things. The 'hard sell' or aggressive tactics rarely work in this modern day and age.

Most positive interactions will lead to a change in perception in both parties.

Force - This is when a persuasive act gains compliance from the other, so they follow the behavior you requested. However, it doesn't change their internal beliefs. It may actually strengthen their beliefs in the opposite direction. This occurs when people are forced or made to do something against their will.

Context - A new behavior may only be relevant within a certain context. For instance, someone may be pressured into arriving at work on time. But will continue to be late for every other appointment they have outside of work. Their inner beliefs around punctuation haven't shifted.

Plurality - This means being able to persuade a number of people at one time.

Presence - When we persuade in person, it is deemed maximum communication since we are present physically. We can also persuade through different means such as e-mail, telephone, social media, letters etc. These methods aren't as influential as physical presence.

Our internal programming's are usually formed as a network of beliefs. The art of persuasion involves breaking and redirecting some of these connections to create a new belief. Sometimes we may have to alter a number of interconnected beliefs before we can change a deep core belief.

Basic Human Needs

From a psychological understanding we know that humans have fundamental needs. This has been defined in many texts none more so than Abraham Maslow's hierarchy of needs. Using this model major corporations and advertising agencies have been able to determine what appeals to the most basic of human needs, so they can increase interest in or sell a particular product. The main emotions these companies focus upon is Safety, Belonging and Esteem (well-being). Since these are basic needs it makes them powerful motivators for advertisers to use. These three emotions are ranked highly in most people's personal value structure. In fact, the more these needs are fulfilled the more happiness and peace we experience in life.

So, by creating a sense of safety, belonging or making people feel important, we open the doors to influencing and persuasion. Here are three simple phrases which help change the way we see things -

1) 'What if' - This phrase takes ego out of the equation and allows people to feel comfortable in creating a safe environment where they can explore deeper feelings and curiosities. 'What if' is a magical phrase and we often hear it from children when they allow their

imaginations to run wild. Used wisely it can be leveraged to open people's minds to new ideas and possibilities. Try asking someone, 'what if you had a million dollars?', they'll tell you more about their real desires and interests than you may have known prior.

2) 'Can you help please?' - This phrase intentionally hands the power to the opposite party. Humans naturally want to help others. By using this statement consciously, we can rely on people's good nature to get us what we want.

3) 'Would it help if' - Similar to example 1, such a statement shifts the focus from a problem to a solution. At the same time using the word 'if', allows the interaction or suggestion to maintain some flexibility. Most of us don't like doing things another person's way but by using the word 'if' we can gradually get others to accept our proposal.

The above three powerful phrases can also work effectively in emails and letters. Simply try using one of these phrases as your email header in the subject line next time you're messaging someone and see how they work for you.

Dale Carnegie the famous author of the book 'How to Win Friends & Influence People' discussed the art of influencing others at great depth. Here is a snippet of some of his main points to winning people over.

1 - The only way to win an argument is to avoid it.

2 - Respect other people's opinions. Be open minded and never say, 'You're wrong.'

3 - If however, you're wrong, don't be afraid of admitting it quickly and emphatically.

4 - Always start an interaction in a friendly way.

5 - Get the opposite party agreeing with you immediately by getting them saying "yes, yes, yes".

6 - Listen intently. Let the other person do most of the talking.

7 - Allow the other person to feel that an idea or suggestion come from them.

8 - Use empathy to see things from the other person's stand point. Acknowledging this perspective, gives us greater power.

9 - Show understanding and sympathy for the other people's ideas and needs.

10 - Make things easier by appealing to people's values and motives.

11 - Set challenges for others. Competitive people naturally welcome challenges. Use this to your advantage. Social - Being Liked

Sociality has a huge impact upon how easily people are influenced. Social proof means how well we are accepted by people and groups, whether personal or professional. How we are influenced in social situations is through three main factors - authority, likability and social proof. We are influenced by authority figures, by the people we like and those who provide us with social proof. For instance, a teenager at school would gain 'social proof' if they were seen mingling with the popular crowd.

Since humans are social creatures, we want to feel connected to one another and as though we're part of something bigger. For this reason, we're more likely to do something simply because we see others doing it. For instance, in a sales negotiation, a company may show a potential new client all the other businesses in the area they deal with. Or in a one-to-one situation we can influence someone by explaining Mr. Popular from another department agreed to it. Knowing others have taken some action before us helps to naturally reduce resistance.

Authority

We're naturally more influenced by those we deem to be above us in some respect. You're more likely to follow directions when they come from management at your place of work rather than if they came from a fellow colleague. We look up too and respect those who are an expert within a certain area or subject, we see these people as an authority.

Something as simple as informing an audience or an individual of your credentials prior to an interaction can help swing the odds into your favor when looking to persuade or influence. This technique can also be effective when emailing, by simply stating at the beginning about any skills you possess in relation to the subject can help make the other person more susceptible to your influence. If for example, you were contacting someone about the possibility of speaking at their event and you had previous experience of speaking at big events, the mere mention of the biggest events you've spoken at, would have an impact on the way the recipient would view your application. We can use this too our advantage and maybe even exaggerate our accomplishments.

Consistency

This is another means of getting people to buy-in to us and is often used as a sales tactic. In this method we ask the target to admit their goals and priorities first and then align our request with their desires. This makes it difficult for them to say no too. Use the information they originally provided and offer them a solution based upon it.

People like to remain consistent and don't like being seen as dishonest, which is why it makes it harder for them to reject a request which matches their needs. When a target shares their goals first, they are invested, once they're invested we can offer the right solutions for them.

Here are a few further strategies which can be used to influence.

This method is named Disrupt and Reframe - This process involves mixing up the words, behaviors or visuals a person is used too and then reframing our pitch/request while they're still trying to figure out the disruption. This method was put to the test by researchers who sold a product giving customers two different options.

The first choice offered - $3 for 8 apples

The second option offered - 300 pennies for 8 apples

The second choice was the clear winner, selling almost twice as many apples as option 1.

This technique works because the target has less resistance to the reframe (option 2) as the brain is thrown off by the initial disruption of the unusual wording.

Storytelling

Another method of getting people onside is through story telling. This enables others to identify with us and the various aspects of our story, which helps build trust. It is important however our story contains the right plot. The three main plots for an influential story are -

1. Challenge Plot - This is the story of the underdog, the rags to riches, the person who made it through some adversity on sheer willpower.

2. Connection Plot - Another common plot, where people build a relationship which

bridges a certain gap. This can be racial, cultural, class, ethnic etc.

3. Creative Plot - This is a story where someone achieves a breakthrough of some sort. Whether solving a long-lasting problem or overcoming an issue in a brand new or innovative way.

If you have any personal stories which you can make meet any of the above criteria, you should find it easier to hook people in.

2. Paradoxical Intervention

This term is simply another way of saying 'Reverse Psychology'. This is a term most of us are familiar with and has been used for years.

Reverse Psychology is a persuasion method that many of us tend to use unconsciously. It involves getting someone to do something we want by suggesting the opposite. This tactic tends to work better when our target is stressed and is making emotional decisions as opposed to thinking things through.

A simple form of reverse psychology is telling someone 'not to do X', by suggesting this we are implanting this very idea into their mind. As we know, children naturally want to do whatever they've been forbidden to do. We can take this further also. If someone commits to something, we can ensure they follow through by expressing doubt over what they have promised. This will make them assert themselves by completing the action in a bid to prove us wrong.

Examples of Reverse Psychology

Here are some basic examples of where we may come across reverse psychology in our day to day life -

A mother suggests to her stingy teenager son, that he can't afford to buy his sister a birthday gift. The boy reacts to this by buying his sister an expensive present.

An office worker who is fed up with a lazy colleague who doesn't pull his weight. May say 'Ok, don't help me. I don't care'. This prompts the colleague to help out.

Or the shy boy who reacts to his friends, who suggest he's not interested in girls, by asking a girl out as his prom date.

Reverse Psychology is more likely to be effective with those who have a desire for control such as rebellious teenagers or type A personalities. They feel that by going against others, they're in control. But we can expose this vulnerability for our own gain.

When someone suggests reverse psychology is being used deliberately. Then reversing the reverse can help. It certainly helps if we act indifferent to whatever decision is made.

One problem with reverse psychology is that if there are other options or alternatives to what we have suggested

the person might choose something else
altogether.

Chapter 5: Managing Your Emotions

Dealing with your feelings is especially an issue of decision. Would you like to, or not? So much has been expounded on feelings and how to manage them adequately, yet numerous individuals can't control this everyday issue. Why? Overseeing feelings viably is really similar to building up an ability or a propensity. It is a method for improving, and as people, we battle with change the most.

Changing the manner in which you generally accomplish something isn't simple and it is much increasingly troublesome with regards to feelings. At the point when we are feeling 'passionate,' the exact opposite thing we need to do is quiet down and attempt to manage the circumstance star effectively; we frequently need to yell about what is upsetting us.

On and when we comprehend somewhat more about how our feelings work, we are in a vastly improved situation to utilize this data to further our potential benefit. Figuring out how to control your feelings can be perhaps the best aptitude you will ever create in your life. Your feelings lead to the moves you make and in this way, make the existence you are encountering now, all aspects of it.

Our enthusiastic piece of the mind, the limbic framework, is perhaps the most established part when looked at, for instance, to our prefrontal cortex, which is our 'thinking' part. Since our enthusiastic part is so old, and in this way an incredibly solid piece of the mind, it is justifiable that it feels like our feelings run us and seize our intuition on occasion. The normal individual's enthusiastic piece of the cerebrum is more than six billion times more dynamic than the prefrontal cortex.

The fact is, your feelings will normally capture your reasoning—this is guaranteed—yet there are still approaches to manage this.

To keep things basic, how about we take a gander at what you can do to flip this circumstance around. Disregarding feelings, stifling them or not managing them will return to haunt you! Stress and uneasiness originate from smothered feelings, so on and when you believe that managing your feelings by disregarding them is getting down to business, you are woefully off-base.

As indicated by numerous neuro phonetic programming methods, there are three components to any expertise or conduct. These 3 components are interconnected and when you change one, you consequently change the others.

To start with, there is the outside conduct which is the thing that the individual really does or says. Furthermore, the individual's inside procedures or musings and thirdly the individual's inward states or feelings. Following are 2 simple and basic approaches to deal with your feelings successfully. Utilize this basic technique to oversee disappointment, outrage, bitterness, dread or some other negative feeling. These are fundamental neuro semantic programming systems.

1. Change your physiology.

Changing your physiology is presumably the least complex neuro etymological programming system to change your feelings in a split second. You can prepare yourself to change your physiology so as to feel certain, excellent, rich, glad, settled or grateful. To do that, become mindful of your physical body when you're miserable, baffled or terrified of something. Is it accurate to say that you are drooped or slouched over? Any tight muscles in your shoulders, back or legs? Are your eyebrows wrinkled, your eyes squinted or perhaps your jaw gripped? At that point, change your physiology immediately, move, lift your hands over your head or bounce around as high as possible. As you do this, see how your feelings and thinking have changed.

2. Change your reasoning.

It's less of what you think yet how you think it. I took in a basic neuro phonetic programming procedure years prior called the cloud method. You can likewise consider it the entryway strategy. Envision 2 entryways or 2 mists before you, one to your left side and one to your right side. At the point when you experience a negative feeling, which is spoken to by a cloud, step away from it (the feeling and the cloud). Ask yourself the 2 after inquiries: does this feeling serve me in that circumstance? Ideally your answer is no. At that point asks yourself: what other helpful feeling I would require in that circumstance. At the point when you think that its, make as though it was the subsequent cloud or the subsequent entryway and start strolling to the entryway or bouncing in the cloud in your creative mind. You just ventured away from a negative feeling and submerged yourself into an increasingly clever state.

With training, you can ace your feelings. It can take you 10 minutes to do it the first run through yet it will just take you seconds with training.

You can't generally control what befalls you, yet you can control your reaction. It isn't tied in with disregarding how you feel, rather you have to comprehend your feelings and utilize this comprehension to pick your reaction to a troublesome circumstance. Doing this work will lessen the impact of weight on your wellbeing, improve your basic leadership and backing everyone around you in accomplishing ideal outcomes.

Here are ten stages to take to deal with your feelings in those profoundly charged minutes.

1. Distinguish and name your feelings. Check in with yourself a few times each day to see how you are feeling. On and when you wind up utilizing general words like fine, OK, or great to portray your feelings, drive yourself to be increasingly explicit and perceive the nuances of your feelings. On and when you can't locate the correct words, possibly you have to grow your passionate jargon. A web search on "arrangements of feelings" will yield arrangements of feelings that you can use as a source of perspective.

2. Recognize feelings and contemplations. Contemplations and feelings are inseparably connected. Much the same as the incredible chicken and egg banter that researchers have had for a considerable length of time it is hard to figure out what starts things out? Yet, our contemplations

do make a passionate encounter. Your contemplations can make physical sensations as your body responds to what you state as though it were genuine. Construct consciousness of your "self-talk" and the physical sensations related with various feelings. This procedure of becoming more acquainted with yourself at an alternate level will fabricate your mindfulness and capacity to deal with your feelings.

3. Skill to quiet yourself down and postpone your response. It might be as straightforward as taking long moderate breaths. The old procedure of tallying to ten really works as a method for quieting enthusiastic responses and giving time for viewpoint. In any event, concentrating on taking notes, or doodling an image for yourself, can be a gainful imaginative discharge. Keep in mind, you have control of your responses. You can't stop the breeze however you can give it a chance to spill off your sails! Before you respond

to a circumstance, give yourself an opportunity to think and pull it together to abstain from saying something that you are probably going to lament.

4. Acknowledge your feelings. Overseeing feelings isn't tied in with passing judgment on a feeling as either fortunate or unfortunate and afterward covering the awful ones. Emotions don't leave since you overlook them. The dreamer technique of disregarding your emotions may give impermanent help yet its conceivable that the sentiments will return considerably more grounded then previously. A little dissatisfaction can prompt outrage or slight worry to freeze. Acknowledge your feelings as data about yourself.

5. Turn the spotlight internal to reflect and get yourself. Consider the circumstances or individuals that annoyed you. Do you see any examples in your responses? Burrow further to comprehend your

responses and hot catches. What are your programmed examples of thought? What suppositions would you say you are making as you make inferences from your perceptions? Are you over-summing up, mind perusing, accusing or foreseeing what's to come. Gain from your reactions and the responses they trigger in others, deciding how you may react in an unexpected way.

6. Build up a propensity for positive self talk. The running critique in your mind is with you day in and day out and can affect your recognitions and frame of mind. In the event that your self talk is negative, it will make your own negative reality. Consider the objectives that you need to accomplish and afterward recognize progressively beneficial musings that help these objectives. Whenever you get yourself in negative self talk, stop and check whether you can re-outline your reasoning utilizing these progressively profitable considerations.

7. Exercise. An extraordinary method to consume off disappointment and stress is work out. Any physical action is a solid outlet for enthusiastic vitality and it will enable your body to be increasingly impervious to push. Start gradually, however have an ordinary program of physical action with the goal that when the weight is on, you are stronger and ready to keep your cool.

8. Express your emotions.....appropriately. Feelings are the magic that binds connections. In the work environment the passionate vitality of the pioneer can help characterize the way of life. Be that as it may, there is a major contrast between conveying everything that needs to be conveyed deferentially and "giving them a chance to have it". Talk and recognize how you feel, however consistently know about the effect on others. Feelings can demolish a culture, or they can help make a working environment that is loaded with vitality,

bounty, good faith, advancement, and trust - prompting achievement.

9. Now and again you simply need to vent. Discharging our feelings can go about as a security valve - easing pressures, much the same as steam out of a pot. On and when you truly need to vent, discover somebody you trust outside the circumstance that will simply hear you out. Perceive that in spite of the fact that blustering may feel great at the time, it is a way to no where, except if you set aside the effort to reflect and comprehend your feelings. Additionally, fuming may simply fan the fire and exacerbate the situation.

10. Practice, practice, practice. The more you practice the means over the more you will flex, manufacture and deal with your enthusiastic muscle.

Dealing with your Emotion

You are better put to deal with your feelings since you realize your issues best.

You have to have the correct instruments that will direct you in realizing how to deal with the feelings in the correct manner. Stress is a condition that influences all individuals from varying backgrounds along these lines, don't believe that there is some kind of problem with you when you wind up focused. There are numerous things that reason pressure and they are generally negative awful things. Remember or compose everything that might be causing your concern. It may be loss of an occupation, loss of a friend or family member, destitution, low self suppositions because of different factors thus substantially more. Keep in mind, there might be more than one stressor at work affecting you to be pushed.

When you have the stressors, you have to neutralize them and start to sustain yourself with inspiration. You may need to leave behind certain organization and a few people wind up leaving a place of employment for their wellbeing.

Remember that the arrangements of a specific issue having a place with someone else won't work for you. You have to encircle yourself with constructive individuals who have a sound point of view. Your feelings are a crucial piece of you and on and when you free the heading of overseeing yourself, your life will likewise be influenced. There are things that will help you mange your feelings viably and they incorporate the accompanying.

You have to give your feelings a chance to direct you or at the end of the day, don't manage to your feelings what you feel. For instance, on and when you are in a distressing circumstance where you believe you have to cry, do no dither. Make your that all your outside elements are working great and they are appropriate this incorporate the suppers that you take in which must be adjusted and sound.

Whenever left unchecked, sentiments can hold us hostage and keep us from encountering genuine joy. Sentiments are genuine, yet we should discover what it is we're truly feeling. We regularly need to make preparations for uncertain feelings from our past that contrarily influences our present circumstance. For instance, in the event that a past relationship left you feeling uncertain and less, at that point certain about yourself, don't extend that feeling into your present relationship.

Outrage and unforgiveness are feelings that stunt us into accepting we're in an ideal situation without the culpable individual. In the event that we harbor outrage, it will obliterate us, frequently prompting forlornness and physiological issues. Despite the fact that we might be defended, it looks bad to enable resentment to control us. You will blow up, however manage it immediately. Try not to allow it to putrefy, causing more harm and a bigger crack in your connections.

Delight, distress, agony, and love are significant notions. God gave us feelings with the goal that we could really react to extraordinary seasons. Feelings are a benchmark for the profound activities of our spirit and enable us to convey what needs be. Feelings have a spot, simply don't give them a chance to manage your life.

Our feelings can serve to lift us to extraordinary statures or thwart our self-improvement. One of the systems which may become helpful with dealing with your feelings is to get careful or mindful of them as they happen. For some individuals, they stay snoozing with regards to the idea of their feelings; the job they serve in their life. Through rehashed presentation of figuring out how to distinguish and deal with your feelings, you have a superior comprehension of how they may best serve you. It requires some investment, persistence and steadiness.

Look at your feelings. What feelings are serving you at the present time? Is it accurate to say that they are helpful? So as to comprehend the feeling and perhaps reframe it, you have to look at the conviction behind it - for that is the fuel. On and when the feeling is one of bitterness, outrage or nervousness, take a gander at whether it is serving your most noteworthy development. The Buddhist guideline states if the feeling isn't vital "drop it - put it down" as if it were a knapsack. It's intended to be as basic as that, yet not exactly so practically speaking.

In the event that you end up becoming violently unhinged when a friend or family member accomplishes an inappropriate thing by you, inspect the feeling. Address it - "what do you need me to know or learn outrage?" Look back to the conviction encompassing the feeling. I can guarantee you that your cherished one isn't the reason or the trigger of your feeling. It's the significance you joined to it when he/she neglected to ring you while they were voyaging interstate on business. You joined an importance and doled out a feeling to it, which served a result - regardless of whether positive or negative.

At the point when you're living in arrangement with your actual self, you build up a profound comprehension and association with self. You're in arrangement with your feelings, contemplations and convictions. They start to serve you, as opposed to neutralize you. You create inward harmony, concordance, satisfaction and ecstasy. You transmit energy, excitement - everyone around you are attracted to you like a moth to a fire. Start now. Take responsibility forever. Put time and persistence in becoming more acquainted with you. You'll pull in the most stunning connections (business, individual, proficient, personal, kinship) and make a real existence deserving of thriving and bounty.

Four basic strides to begin controlling your feelings adequately.

1. The First Step Is Awareness

On and when you don't know about the occasions when you are excessively enthusiastic or going overboard, how might you attempt to oversee it? It is unimaginable. Begin to screen your feelings and offer names to them. Now and then we think that its hard to recognize what we are feeling. Giving it a name encourages us gain lucidity, which is fundamental in pushing ahead.

2. Find the 'Why' of Your Emotions

When you have recognized how you are feeling, you need to find why you are feeling it. What is causing this inclination inside you? Obviously, there could be a million reasons, and to discover you need to ask yourself, similar to you would a companion, "What's going on? What is making me feel along these lines?" Your mind will consistently search for an answer.

More often than not, just the manner in which you are considering the circumstance is making you feel the manner in which you do. Another colossal motivation behind why we feel negative feelings is on the grounds that our qualities are absent at that time or being regarded.

Keep in mind: find the 'why.'

3. At that point Ask Yourself, "What Is the Solution?"

When you have found why, what would you be able to do to reclaim control? Some of the time, you may need to change the manner in which you are pondering the circumstance.

Your contemplations lead legitimately to your sentiments; so in the event that you are feeling terrible, you no doubt have a negative idea that is making you feel that way. On and when you start considering other potential methods for taking a gander at the circumstance, you will start to feel better right away. What you center around grows!

Now and again, by essentially understanding why you feel a specific route at a specific time, your feelings will begin to decrease since seeing consistently prompts quieting.

4. Pick How You Want to React

This is the hardest part. The manner in which that we respond and deal with our feelings is a propensity. Haven't you seen those individuals who get worried about nothing, actually blowing a gasket at nothing? You nearly feel frustrated about them. They have made a propensity for partner a circumstance they don't care for with 'going ballistic.' Their feelings have seized them.

Figuring out how to tune in to your feelings, to distinguish, comprehend and afterward pick them, isn't something that you choose to rehearse two times per week at noon. No, it is with constant exertion and control that you can begin to fabricate this basic aptitude.

9 Simple Tips to Help You Manage Your Emotions

As a therapist, given a ton of thought to how to have a more advantageous existence by dealing with your feelings. Here are a portion of my considerations, which I communicated in my book, "The Emotional Revolution."

Feelings can have a significant impact on physical wellbeing, and it is basic to manage the emotions that go with the ordinary good and bad times of life.

9 Steps to Help Manage Your Emotions:

1. Utilize your feelings and substantial reactions to perceive when you are under pressure. A hustling beat, dry mouth, hurting stomach, tight muscles, or muscle torment may all demonstrate that something is out of order in your passionate world.

2. Record your considerations and emotions about what is focusing on you. Take a day by day stock of your feelings. By recording what you feel and when, you might have the option to recognize examples of passionate high points and low points. On and when is additionally imperative to record the musings that go with the emotions.

3. Control whatever part of the pressure that you can. Life presents numerous circumstances consistently, and you ought

not see them in high contrast terms-those you can control versus those you can't. Search for the shades of dark the components you can control. At the point when you realize what will occur in a circumstance, you sensory system can equip to deal with it.

4. Try not to make mountains out of molehills. At the point when troublesome circumstances emerge, it is essential to survey how terrible they truly are before going into alarm mode. On and when you need to carry on with a low-stress life, don't get all worked up over minor issues.

5. Reclassify the Problem. Your demeanor to stress can influence your wellbeing beyond what the pressure itself can. In the event that the issue is out of your control, perceive that and rethink the issue to figure out which parts you can maintain a strategic distance from or handle.

6. Create practices that occupy you from stress. Anything you do that diverts you from your worry for some time is great. For instance, go for a stroll or work in the nursery.

7. Connect with a companion of relative. Social connections are useful for your wellbeing, and contacting somebody about your pressure can improve your standpoint. On and when you are deficient with regards to informal communities, you may think that its most straightforward to meet others during a mutual movement.

8. Exercise Regularly. Standard practice is useful for your physical and enthusiastic wellbeing. Indeed, even moderate exercise can help decrease pressure.

9. Ponder and Relax. Reflection has a wide assortment of medical advantages, and stress decrease is one of the enormous ones.

5 Tips in Managing Emotions

Avoid Triggers

You thought this enthusiastic thing was simple, correct? Award it, for certain individuals it is simple. There are individuals who are commonly laid back and have an idea about this enthusiastic thing. Bravo, however for all of us, we have to choose our fights. Focus on what triggers you. Is it somebody taking your parking spot, or somebody who didn't state "thank you" for a blessing? You are not supporting the conduct, you are simply going to maintain a strategic distance from circumstances or have a procedure to proceed onward. Pick another stopping place, have a reinforcement, or in the event of the discourteous blessing taker, center around the part of giving without getting something back like a "much obliged."

Avoid Jumping the Gun

Try not to respond immediately as this will put you on the way of conceivable obliteration. Settle on the choice to do nothing until you have chilled off. Leave for a minute and inhale profound for five minutes the Huffington Post shared. "Keep on breathing profoundly for five minutes, feeling as your muscles untense and your pulse comes back to ordinary." Feel better? If not, devise an arrangement early on what should be possible to occupy you from the pressure. Go for a stroll, supplicate, go have some espresso, or play music. Acknowledge that you can't control every one of the difficulties throughout everyday life, except you can control the manner in which you respond to them.

Be Optimistic

Be an individual who is idealistic and change your mentality. This will help with unpleasant circumstances and help to adapt to wild feelings. We realize pressure is unsafe to our wellbeing. In the event that we are increasingly idealistic about existence, we will live more advantageous lives. Start with positive self-talk. This not exclusively will support feelings, the body, however the psyche. It could help with wretchedness, lessen strain, and decrease the danger of cardiovascular sicknesses. Changing your reasoning presently will pay for itself later as the psyche and feelings are associated. Saddle musings and discharge them when they are dangerous. Attempt music, nature, or a side interest to have an outlet when life gets to you. By and large, by turning out to be progressively idealistic and positive we

Be Grateful

Be appreciative and think about the beneficial things throughout everyday life. This will help quiet you down and will direct your mind-set. Appreciation takes your brain off yourself and celebrates what you as of now have. It can likewise enable forlornness, to bring down hostility and help with melancholy. Have a go at excusing yourself after you fall away from overseeing feelings, you are just human. It will be a procedure. Advise yourself that easy-going others will likewise enable you to pick appreciation, as opposed to nourishing into negative feelings, particularly after you feel insulted. In the event that this is still difficult to do, connect with a companion to keep you responsible and to enable you to vent.

Letting Go

There are more significant things in life than cutoff times, work, satisfying individuals, and having feelings that standard you. See the master plan and that your feelings are short lived. Stop the hyper center around circumstances that are bothering. We need to not give it a chance to affect us hours after the fact. Release it. Releasing the feelings is startling as it is a demonstration of give up, and we feel that we are being aloof, yet this isn't valid. Dropping the offense can be seen as an activity - a change we as a whole can partake in. It's fine to cry or hit a pad out of dissatisfaction. We have to have an arrival of negative sentiments as it is solid.

Chapter 6: How To Protect Yourself From Manipulation

Manipulation commonly occurs when an individual is used for the benefit of others. It is a situation where the manipulator comes up with an imbalance of power and goes ahead to exploit his victim just to serve their main agendas. Those who are manipulative are the kind of people who will disguise their desires and interests as yours. They will undertake all they can to make you believe that their own opinions are the objective facts. They will then act as if they are cornered. Manipulators will pretend to offer assistance to improve your attitude, performance and promise that they will help you improve your life in general. That is all that they want you to believe. The hidden truth is that these people's main aim is to control you and not control you, as they want you to feel. They are not interested in making your life better, but just to change you. They also want to validate their lives and make sure that you don't outgrow them.

Once you have given these characters back to your life, getting rid of them will not be easy. They will appear to flip flop on issues and act so slippery when you want to hold them accountable. They also tend to promise you help that doesn't seem to be near.

People can be manipulated when they opt to put up with passive-aggressive behaviors. According to a recent study published in the Journal of Social & Personal Relationships, offensive people tend to interfere with an individual's general performance. The study also noted that ignoring those who are negative could do you more harm than good. When these people are ignored, the research states that their productivity and intelligence is increased. Over 100 participants were examined for this study. Participants were asked to ignore or talk with random people who is either offensive or friendly.

The participants were not aware of the kind of people they were going to meet. After interacting for about four minutes, each participant was offered a thought exercise that needed them to have a better concentration. The study later noted that those who ignored the malicious individuals performed way much better than those who engaged them.

The researchers then summarized that ignoring some people in severe social interaction is one better way of conserving a person's mental resources. The best strategy is to avoid those who are negative in their speeches and actions. But at times, that can't be enough. A cynical person can also be manipulative and sneaky at times. In such situations, you will try to apply other strategies.

The truth is that being manipulated is not a good thing. The only possible worse thing than manipulation could just be admitting our dirty little secrets. Each time we realize that we have been manipulated, we feel stupid and ashamed and weak. And all that doesn't stop there. If we continue to fall for the tricks that these people lay on us, they will leave us with an awful feeling about everything around us. Instead of being hurt for another time, the best thing to do could just be not to trust anybody.

Manipulation can only be successful if the target fails to recognize it or just decide to allow it. But regardless of all that, there exist certain things that you can do to acknowledge that you are under manipulative powers. They can also help you to prevent or stop a possible case of manipulation. Some of the ideas may not be desirable or possible for your situation, but that's just fine because every situation and every person is different.

Know all your fundamental rights

One of the single most imperative guidelines when you are in this similar situation is to know all your fundamental rights. But that's not all. You should also recognize when there is a violation of any of those rights. Remember that you are at liberty to stand up for yourself and ensure no single breach of fundamental rights. You should, however, do this carefully and make sure that you do not harm others. Again, you should not forget that you might forfeit these rights if you cause harm to other people. Ensure you are conversant with some of the fundamental human rights such as:

The right

to be treated with dignity and respect.

To express one's wants, opinions, and feelings.

To give no as an answer and maintain that without any guilty feelings.

To set up one's standards and priorities.

To take care and safeguard yourself from being emotionally, mentally, or physically threatened.

The mentioned fundamental rights show the extent to which your boundaries are supposed to reach. We are living in a society where people don't represent any of these rights. The mental manipulators are particularly interested in depriving you of your rights so that they can fully control you and take advantage of you. However, you still have the moral authority and power to state that you are entirely in charge of your life and not the manipulator.

Maintain a distance from these people

As noted, one of the surest ways of detecting a manipulator is to check if the individual acts with different faces when in front of various people and situations. Whereas all of us have mastered this art of social differentiation, the mental manipulators are masters when it comes to dwelling in extremes – where they show great humility to one person and rude to the other. They can also feel so aggressive at one point and helpless the next minute. When you see this kind of behavior in people you are close to, the best thing to do is keep a healthy distance. You should also try to avoid engaging with these people until you are compelled to do that. Remember that some of the top causes of chronic psychological manipulation are deep-seated and complex; therefore, saving or changing these people cannot be your job.

Stop Self-Blaming & Personalization

Given that the manipulator plans to know where your weakness is and exploit it, you may even throw the blame game on yourself for not doing your best. It is imperative to reassure yourself that you are not part of the problem in such situations. Remember that you are just being manipulated to feel bad about your actions and surrender your rights and power in the end. It is vital to consider the kind of relationship you have with the manipulator as well. These are some of the questions that you should ask yourself:

Am I getting respectful treatment?

Is this relationship 1-way or 2-way?

Am I satisfied being in this relationship?

The answers to these issues will offer you the most important clues about whether the problem is with the manipulator or you.

Probe the Manipulators

Mental manipulators will always make demands or requests from you. They do this to make you go the extra mile so that you can meet their needs. At times, it can be essential to focus on the manipulator each time you hear specific solicitations. Ask them some analytical questions to check if they are fully aware of their scheme's inequity. Ask them if their actions appear reasonable to them or if what they want from you is all fair.

When you step out to ask some of these questions, you are merely placing a mirror so the manipulator will be able to view the real nature of his/her ploy. If the manipulator happens to be a master of self-awareness, then he/she will withdraw and back down. On the other hand, real pathological manipulators will dismiss the question and insist on doing their way. When this takes place, ensure you stand up for your fundamental rights, and the manipulators will flee.

Say No in a Firm and Diplomatic Way

Saying no is a firm and diplomatic way of what is defined as real communication. It will allow you to stand your ground and maintain the best working relationship after sufficient articulation. It is important to remember that one of your fundamental human rights is to set your standards and priorities. It is also within your rights to say no without feeling guilt, as well as the right to pick your own healthy and happy life.

Set the Consequences

When a mental manipulator persists in violating the boundaries you have made and is not hearing your "no," you will be forced to deploy the consequences. The ability to point out and assert the products is one of the essential skills you can deploy to resist a manipulative person's efforts. When they are articulated effectively, results will stop the manipulative person's actions and even compel them to stop the violations and respect instead.

Confront the Bullies in a Safe Way

One fact that is unknown to many is that a mental manipulator can turn into a bully when they intimidate and harm others. It is important to note that bullies only prey on those they regard as the weakest, and you can make yourself a target when you remain compliant and passive. However, the fact is that many bullies are cowards on the inside. They will often back up when their target starts to stand up for their rights. It is a common practice in office and surroundings, as well as in schoolyards.

Think about the long-term consequences of the actions you undertake

As opposed to just doing what is most comfortable and fastest, do not forget about your actions' consequences. Remember that psychological manipulators are the best for making their options the most comfortable, most rapid, and the least hurtful. They are also best at keeping the people focused on their current feelings. That explains why people do things they later regret. Instead of dealing with a consequence, later on, make sure you choose to do something that you won't be forced to rethink.

Chapter 7: Understand Human Psychology

Psychology is generally accepted as the scientific study of the mind and human behavior. It focuses on the mind, how the mind functions, and also how it influences or affects behavior. "Psychology" is a word that comes from the Greek words "psyche" and "logo." Psyche means or translates to "life," while logos means "explanation."

The mind is very complex, and so are the things that are related to it, which can make it hard to treat. Psychology encompasses all facets of the human experience, ranging from the workings and functions of the brain to the decisions and actions of nations. This even includes the development of a child and the care given or received by the aged. It encompasses the process of thoughts, memories, emotions, dreams, behavior, perception, and many more that cannot be physically seen but understood.

The subject psychology covers the study of both the conscious and the unconscious occurrences including thought and feeling. Psychology is also an academic discipline with a very broad scope. It pursues the understanding of the evolving properties and workings of the brain. As a social science, psychology pursues the understanding of both groups and individuals by researching particular cases and instituting broad-spectrum principles.

A psychologist is a professional researcher or practitioner in any field of psychology, and they are classified as behaviorists, cognitive psychologists, or social scientists. Psychologists aim to understand the function of the human mind, behavior, and mental processes ranging from attention, cognition, perception, intelligence, emotions, phenomenology, brain-functioning, decision-making, morality, relationships, motivation, and even personality.

Psychology has been acclaimed to be the "core science." In medical science, it leans toward psychiatry and neurology, while in the social sciences, it leans toward human behavior, development, experiences, and other subdisciplines within psychology.

Although psychological knowledge is habitually used for the assessment and treatment of issues related to mental health, it is also applied every day in several other spheres of human endeavors. This includes understanding and solving different types of problems, such as solving mysteries and problems in crime dramas on television. Psychology, in the long run, aims to benefit and advance society.

Most psychologists are engaged in different roles, from practicing in clinics, managing a therapeutic practice, counseling, or practicing in school settings. Other psychologists engage in a wide range of scientific research covering broad areas such as mental processes and behavior. Some provide services to psychology departments in universities, including teaching hospitals and medical schools. Other psychologists are employed to provide professional services in large organizations and in government settings. Finally, other settings where you might find a psychologist include a forensic investigation department, law agencies, human development and aging, media, health, and sports as well as in the military and intelligence.

Emotions

Our emotions appear to be in control of our daily lives. The decisions we make are based on whether we are sad, happy, angry, frustrated, or bored. The hobbies and activities we choose to partake in are incited by our emotions. Moving through our daily lives, we get to experience a variety of emotions.

What are emotions? Emotions are complex psychological states that encompass three different components: a subjective experience, a behavioral or expressive response, and a physiological response. Adding to the definition of emotions, researchers have been able to identify and classify emotions into types.

However, these descriptions and insights appear to be changing over time.

Emotion is a subjective state of being, which we often describe as feelings. Emotion and mood are sometimes used interchangeably, but psychologists have pointed out that these words mean two different things. Basically, the word emotion denotes a subjective affective state which is relatively intense and occurs in response to what we experience. Emotions are experienced intentionally and consciously. On the other hand, mood refers to a less intense, prolonged, affective state which doesn't occur in response to what we experience. The state of mood may not be consciously experienced and may not carry the consciousness/intentionality that is associated with emotion. In this section, we will be focusing on human emotion.

Our emotions are essential to our ability to adapt to life's challenges. When we have a good feeling, we are able to shrug off even the biggest of tasks, but when we feel troubled or worried, we tend to see an enjoyable task as too burdensome and view it with a sense of doom and gloom. Our emotions can even go beyond and affect our relationships with other people. For example, if a friend is telling you a sad story and expects you to respond looking sad or concerned, but you choose to look unconcerned and snicker instead, you will only appear rude and insensitive. Likewise, if you are frowning when a friend is telling you of a very funny joke, you will also appear offensive and uninterested.

Going off the handle just because of a minor annoyance can make you appear unbalanced or too hyper.

If you give an undue happy reaction to information tagged as good news, people will start to question your stability and maturity. If it was a baby, they are totally allowed to wail with rage and shriek with pleasure at any time, but as an adult, people expect you to rein in the outward expression of your feelings.

Our emotions play an important role in our ability to succeed or fail in the challenges thrown at us. Just think about the famous people whose careers have taken a step back because of the way their feelings were expressed. For example, during the primary run-up to the 2004 United States presidential election, the candidacy of Howard Dean ended overnight after his "YAAAAHHH" moment became an internet frenzy.

Prior to that, Edmund Muskie made the same political blunder during the 1972 primary season. Muskie shed tears after he won the New Hampshire primary. However, he claimed the tears were snowflakes that were shimmering in the morning light. In the same light, Hillary Clinton wasn't seen as a sympathetic fellow until she had her eyes wet when answering a voter's question. Of course, some pundits used that act against her and questioned her sincerity. You might be asking what these examples have to do with the role of emotions in our lives.

The above examples show us that the outward display of our inner feelings has the power to influence how we are treated by others. Meanwhile, these emotional displays are greatly dependent on our cultural norms. To be recognized as a well-adapted member of society, it is important that we adhere to the norms or risk ridicule or condemnation from other people.

According to the findings of psychologist Paul Ekman in 1972, there are six basic emotions that are recognized widely. These are happiness, sadness, fear, anger, surprise, and disgust. The way in which people express these emotions differs quite radically based on the norms of everyone's culture. In 1999, Ekman expanded his list of basic emotions and included a number of others, including excitement, embarrassment, contempt, pride, shame, amusement, and satisfaction.

Prominent psychologist Robert Plutchik also introduced an emotion classification he called the "wheel of emotions." This model of emotion classification shows how different emotion types can be combined or mixed together just like a color wheel where primary colors are mixed to make other colors.

Chapter 8: What Is Mental Manipulation

Manipulation is a type of social influence in which the goals are to alter others' behavior or perception using techniques, either direct or indirect. Some techniques may be considered handed; some may not.

Such techniques could be regarded as exploitative and devious by promoting the manipulator's interests, often at another's cost.

Although social influence or impact may represent underhanded manipulation depending on context and motivations, the concept of exercise is not necessarily negative of social influence. Use basic tools to your advantage. Ask inquisitive questions, take advantage of time, don't allow yourself to take the blame, and be polite but firm.

Asking questions is a good way to take the attention from you back to your manipulator. This can be frustrating for them because they don't expect you to ask your questions, especially if they have already been manipulating you. It's a good way to fluster them and make them aware of their own game. They will have to regroup or turn the tables and use another tactic on you, so be aware.

When you are being manipulated or if someone is attempting to get you to do something, you can easily put them off by saying something along the lines of, "I'll have to think about it." On a normal basis, your manipulator expects you not to think but do. This can stir them up a bit and confuse them when you don't jump to their demands.

Avoiding people or situations that make you uncomfortable is also another way to deal with manipulation. If you know a person is manipulating, you stay away from them at least until you can either take control or ignore their tactics. If there are certain places where you feel uncomfortable where there are people who try to get you to do things you don't want to, stay away from that place. It will make life a lot less stressful if you follow your instincts and stay away.

One of the target's biggest issues is blaming or feeling as if something is wrong with them. This is what a manipulator wants. If you can be positive and disallow yourself in believing the things the manipulator tries to convince you of, then you are one step ahead of them.

No matter what they say, you have to take a step back and believe in yourself. Have the positivity that overpowers their negative energy. Allow their remarks and actions to wash over you without allowing them to soak in.

Things to Keep in Mind About Your Manipulator

Most Generally, They Are Just Bullies

Usually, a manipulator will back down if you begin to put your foot down. They like passive and compliant people, those easy to control. Once it isn't easy, they will most likely give up.

A lot of time, your manipulator is a victim as well, and this is how they cope. Now that doesn't make it right, but maybe it makes it a little more understanding. Someone who doesn't have any control in their life or is being abused wants to find their power. They search for someone they consider weaker than they are and target them. It makes them feel stronger and less vulnerable.

Other times none of this is the case, and they are what they are: manipulators through and through. You cannot change them, but you can overpower them and disallow them to control you.

Once you have taken control you need to set boundaries. Boundaries are important, especially for people you have no choice but to deal with regularly. You don't have the luxury of totally taking them out of your life. If this is the case keeping your boundaries and setting consequences for them crossing the boundaries is important. This shows them that you are serious and may make them rethink you as a weak individual. But be consistent. Just like a child, if you slip up even once, your manipulator will take that as a free pass and continue to push the limits. What is Manipulation?

Manipulation deals with using your actions, mannerisms, hands, and even other parts of your body to get someone to do what you want or to shape a situation to your desire. You could think of it as selfish, but I tell you that there is a drive-in for every wrongdoing. Therefore, the drive behind manipulation could be positively used. An instance can be seen in how a good DJ tries to bring different music modes together to display his skills in bringing many tunes together into a lovely mix of sounds to the audience. We could say this is almost unfair to the original artist of each song. Also, someone that is good at manipulating would know how to do so in words, emotions, and feelings to the very end of getting his or her main desire.

The practice of manipulation could involve using an indirect scheme and plan to be in charge of relationships. Periodic manipulation involves telling a friend that he or she is looking well when the person is actually mentally depressed or/and physically down. This is quite technical as it will affect your friend's perceptions of you, which will eventually translate to how the person relates to you. Emotional abuse can be associated with manipulation, especially when it is experienced in very close relationships. Depending on the point of view, someone can consider manipulation negative when the person being manipulated is affected physically, emotionally, or mentally while another person can argue that because being manipulative helps to put one's surroundings and environment, including people, into subjection and under control. Moreover, manipulators could find it hard to connect with their original selves, and being manipulated can lead to ill effects on an individual.

To understand manipulation, you have to identify the three major distinct types. First, we have manipulation of options in which the options available in the environment are modified by rewards or threats. The second one is the manipulation of information; here the individual's way of perceiving things is modified such that the understanding of the situation gets affected. Also, psychological manipulation is a process of influencing someone such that there is a change in mental cognition.

During manipulative encounters, there are four main components of manipulations, which are hearer, motive, covertness, and interest of the speaker. These are usually referred to as prerequisites to manipulation. Any form of manipulation is geared towards affecting a hearer or victim. The target often times will behave in such a way to oppose how he acts before being manipulated. Actually, in a manipulative situation, the manipulator has a larger vision spectrum, which means that the manipulator knows much better than the target.

Talking about motive, is this not what characterizes manipulation itself? The intention of the speaker determines to what extent the target is manipulated. However, this intention cannot be known it would be self-defeating. There is usually a communication involving the hearer, the speaker, and the speaker's communicated motives.

For the widespread view on manipulation to hold, it then needs to remain covert. I can assume to a large extent that the motive of the speaker is one important feature in manipulation. It is designed to suit the desire and interest of the speaker. I can also tell you that there is a correlation between a manipulative mechanism and the manipulator's motive.

It is imperative to know that manipulations can be done unconsciously or without being aware, while some manipulate deliberately. Intentional manipulators are tricky. They would even brag about what they do because they are very much aware. The game known as manipulation enables manipulators to be wise, smart, and cunny at the same time. They are also self-centred, so you cannot claim to be good at manipulating and care for others.

Various Forms of Manipulation

• Unintentional resistance to others' demands can be making excuses, blaming others, sarcasm, hiding anger, among others.

• Indirect or Implied Threats. An example of this is when, as a mother, you give your child a bad look for dropping his or her dirty uniform on the floor.

• Deceitfulness in character or behavior includes cheating, fabrication, corruption, and even stealing.

• Selfishness in disseminating useful information. For example, you have a friend that needs a job as you are, and where you get information about companies having vacancies, you hold it back from him or her.

• She is making someone leave a company or association of loved ones. A single mother could fall into this category. Because of hatred from the child's father, she isolates the child from the father and his family, who truly loves him.

• Attempt to destabilize someone's belief. This often leads to misdirection, denial, and low self-esteem.

• Forcefully criticizing, insulting, or denouncing another person. A typical example is bullying

• Achieving a goal via sexual intercourse. This is common among employers and employees.

However, if manipulation is not being addressed, people who are being manipulated can suffer from poor mental health. Chronic manipulation could result in depression, anxiety, wrong coping methods, lying, and difficulty trusting people. It could also make a victim lose his or her value system and doubt things in their real sense. An instance was illustrated in a classic movie titled Gaslight, wherein in a subtly manner, the husband of a woman manipulated her until she no longer depends on how she perceives things. The man secretly turned down the gaslights, and he made his wife believe that the way the light looks dim was all in her head.

Manipulators are also good at saying sweet things their victims would like, and most words from them are not all that true. They take advantage of being skilled in this to develop a close and amazing connection with people. A manipulator will deliberately create an imbalanced way of using a victim to their advantage. Until such a person gets what he/she wants, they can go to any length.

There is some subtle behavior that you should smell manipulation when you sense them either from you or others. Instances include acting dumb and pretending to be nice and lovely all the time. If we all what to be truthful, at a point or the other in our lives, we have been manipulative. Sometimes, to control people, tell a lie to get out of a situation or even flatter. To some people, it is a way of life.

As you know, or have even experienced, manipulators are everywhere and around us. The question should be, what personalities do they possess? A manipulator could be your next-door friend who spreads gist and gossip about you. They could even be your family members who make people around them feel insecure or who always create chaos, so in the end, anybody could manipulate you. On the road, manipulators are usually criminals who rely on gimmicks to distract you from taking your belongings.

Chapter 9: What Is Persuasion And Influence

There are many times when the human mind is pretty easy to influence, but it does take a certain set of skills to get people to stop and listen to you. Not everyone is good with influence and persuasion, though. They can talk all day and would not be able to convince others to do what they want. On the other hand, some could persuade anyone to do what they want, even if they had just met this person for the first time. Knowing how to work with these skills will make it easier for you to recognize a manipulator and be better prepared to avoid them if needed.

The first thing that we need to look at is what persuasion is. Persuasion is simply the process or action taken by a person or a group of people when they want to cause something to change. This could be with another human being and something that changes in their inner mental systems or their external behavior patterns.

The act of persuasion, when it is done properly, can sometimes create something new within the person, or it can just modify something already present in their minds. Three different parts come with the process of persuasion including:

• The communicator or other source of the persuasion

• The persuasive nature of the appeal

• The audience or the target person of the appeal

All three elements must be taken into consideration before you try to do any form of persuasion on your own. You can just look around at the people who are in your life, and you will probably be able to see some types of persuasion happening all over the place.

The above options are all positive ways that you can use persuasion to your advantage. Most people will be amenable to these happening. But on the other side, there are four negative tactics of persuasion that you can do as well. These would include options like manipulating, avoiding, intimidating, and threatening. These negative tactics will be easier for the target to recognize, which is why most manipulators will avoid using them if possible.

Now, you can use some of the tactics above. Still, according to psychologist Robert Cialdini, six major principles of persuasion can help you to get the results that you want without the target being able to notice what is going on. Let us take a look at these six weapons and how they can be effective.

The six weapons of influence

Reciprocity

The first principle of persuasion that you can use is known as reciprocity. This is based on the idea that when you offer something to someone, they will feel a bit indebted to you and will want to reciprocate it back. Humans are wired to be this way to survive. For the manipulator to use this option, they will make sure that they are doing some kind of favor for their target. Whether that is paying them some compliments, giving them a ride to work, helping out with a big project or getting them out of trouble. Once the favor is done, the target will feel like they owe a debt to the manipulator. The manipulator will then be able to ask for something, and it will be really hard for the target to say no.

Commitment and consistency

It is like humans to settle for what is already tried and tested in the mind. Most of us have a mental image of who we are and how things should be. And most people are not going to be willing to experiment, so they will keep on acting the way that they did in the past. So, to get them to work with this principle and do what you want, you first need to get them to commit to something. The steps that you would need to follow to get your target to do what you want through commitment and consistency includes:

• Start out with something small. You can ask the target to do something small, something that is easier to manage the change, before they start to integrate it more into their personality and get hooked on the habit.

• You can get the target to accept something publicly so that they will feel more obligated to see it through.

• Reward the target when they can stick to the course. Rewards will be able to help strengthen the interest of the target in the course of action that you want them to do.

Social proof

This is another one that will rely on the human tendency, and it relies on the fact that people place a lot of value and trust in other people and in their opinions on things that we have not tried yet. This can be truer if the information comes from a close friend or a person who is perceived as the expert. It is impossible to try out everything in life and having to rely on others can put us at a disadvantage. This means that we need to find a reliable source to help us get started. A manipulator may be able to get someone to do something by acting as a close friend or an expert. They are able to get the target to try out a course of action because they have positioned themselves as the one who knows the most about the situation or the action.

Influence is a powerful, but often subtle tool. The ability to affect or change someone's opinion, or create a change in circumstances without forcing the change directly is an art form all its own. Creating changes or conditions as situations develop creates lasting impact. It can make others sit up and take notice of you and your presence, and often create a perception of you that may make others want to defer to you in the future. We will go over how to create influence, how to build your skills in regards to influencing others, and how to utilize the influence you have built to achieve your goals.

Influence is based on basic, but key factors. Let's start with a room full of people whom you do not know. Your entrance into this room is vital. You may not know anyone, but not everyone present will know this. Presenting yourself in the most flattering way within the first few seconds will often dictate the way everyone in the room sees you. Smile as you enter the room, walking with your back and head in straight but relaxed alignment. Taking time not to rush or enter too slowly, imagine you are just walking into a room in your home. An often-effective trick to make you seem more approachable is to give a short wave, as if you are acknowledging someone you know. This makes others assume that someone else in the room already knows you and that in and of itself makes you seem more likeable or interesting.

When first meeting someone, making eye contact and firmly shaking their hand while smiling boosts your effective charisma with the other individual. Charisma is more about how you make the other person feel when they are in your presence. Charisma is not necessarily about being the life of the party. To work on your charisma, first consider your own strengths. Are you humorous? Are you already outgoing and friendly? Do you tend to be shy and quieter? You can use any of your strengths to your advantage; it is all about understanding how to use them. If you are more of an introvert, pick one or two people off to the side of the crowd or room to engage with. When initiating communication, use your quieter presence to let others do more of the talking, and only steer the conversation in the direction you want it to go into when necessary. People love to talk about themselves! If you are outgoing, place yourself in a position of power, feel free to approach larger groupings of people and greet them. Again, use your strengths to your advantage.

People that hold sway over others can attest, influence is all about give and take. When people feel, a relationship is based on reciprocation, they trust the relationship easier and sooner, and have fewer reservations. Try asking a small favor of someone, and then in turn offering them the same in return. An example would be offering to hold someone's place in line while they use the restroom, taking notes for them while they excuse themselves momentarily during a meeting or presentation, and then asking them to do the same for you upon their return. This give and take lays a foundation of comradery, like you and the other party are already friendly. And people that feel like you like them, like you in return.

Building relationships overnight is not easy, but it can be easier by being friendly. Smiling and eye contact play a role in how you make other people feel. If you project that you are happy to see others that you are happy to be speaking with them, they will in turn feel happy to be communicating with you. Your body language speaks volumes, and others pick up on what you are conveying with yours, even if they aren't fully aware of it. When engaging with another, take note in how they are standing or sitting. If they are standing with their arms at their sides, you should mimic their stance. Mimicking someone's body language is another way of building an unspoken but solid foundation. If they are clearly exhibiting stress, mimic their stance. An example of this would be if their arms are crossed over the front of their body in defensive pose. After a few minutes of conversation, move your arms to a more relaxed and natural position. In most instances, the person you are communicating with will subconsciously reposition their body language to mimic your own. This is an example of how you are already gaining influence and trust with someone who you barely know.

When talking to individuals you want to gain influence over, another aspect to consider is your own attitude towards them. We know that our physical body language plays a role, and that reciprocating is important as well, but just as important is how you project yourself. Greeting another with a smile is great, but now that the conversation has started, maintains a neutral but relaxed facial expression. Staying involved and being attentive when others speak again makes them feel good speaking with you. Asking questions per the flow of conversation shows that you are listening to them, and everyone wants to be heard. Being respectful, calm, and diplomatic in your interactions makes you more friendly and approachable. Showing gratitude for their time, and being appreciated will encourage others to appreciate your attention and time in return.

Chapter 10: The History Of Reading Body Language

Body language encompasses the gestures and motions we can interpret in order to make sense of someone else's emotions or feelings. These cues consist of posture, gestures, facial expressions, use of space and touch. Both human beings and animals make use of body language as a means of communication, though early human beings definitely relied more heavily on this form of communication than modern man.

Nobody is absolutely sure whether we are born with the ability to read body language or whether we acquire the ability as we grow up, however, most people are capable—at least at some level—of reading and interpreting body language. The reason why nobody is really sure how we acquire this ability is two-fold. Firstly, body language can be divided into numerous categories. Some of our body language is inborn, like scowling when you are angry, while other pieces are cultural and learned through observation (for example, in some African cultures it is considered rude to look an authority figure in the eye, while in the Western world, avoiding eye contact is generally considered to be a sign that a person is being deceitful). Secondly, scientists are still trying to figure out why some aspects of body language evolved and for what reason.

The study of body language, known as kinesics, probably started with Francis Bacon, an English philosopher who lived between 1561 and 1626. In 1605, in his novel Of the Proficience of Advancement and Learning, Human and Divine, Bacon posited that a great deal of the communication that occurs between human beings is done through gestures.

After Bacon, however, the study of body language went dormant for many years.

That is, until Charles Darwin came along. Darwin lived between 1809 and 1882, and was most well-known for his theories on evolution. But Darwin dabbled in psychology, too. Many, many years after Darwin's death, a professor named Peter Snyder came across an archive of an experiment Darwin had conducted on facial expressions. This experiment was inspired after Darwin and French physician, Guillame-Benjamin-Amand Duchenne, had spent some time exchanging letters. Duchenne believed that that 60 distinct expressions could be produced by the human face, and that there were specific muscle groups which controlled each expression. Darwin disagreed. Darwin thought that there were far fewer expressions, and that many different muscles work together to control each expression.

To test his hypothesis, Darwin showed pictures of human facial expressions to 11 test subjects and asked them to identify the underlying emotion. Not surprisingly, his notes seemed to indicate that most of the respondents were able to positively identify emotions like anger, happiness, fear, shock, and excitement based off of the pictures Darwin had displayed.

The next prominent scientist to consider body language was Margaret Mead, in 1977. Mead lived between 1901 and 1978, and served as the president of the American Association for the Advancement of Science during her lifetime. She believed that body language was culture specific (and thus that it did not have an inborn component).

Mead's contemporary, Paul Ekman, was born in 1934. In the mid-1960s, Ekman launched a study into whether body language was universal or culture-specific. With over 40 years of research, Ekman's prevailing consensus remains that certain facial expressions are universal, and thus are inborn. Ekman's studies with Wallace Friesen support this hypothesis, amongst others.

Desmond Morris, the famous zoologist and author of The Naked Ape, was born in 1928 in Wiltshire, England. He believed that body language primarily evolved to meet the challenges of prehistoric life as a hunter. One of Morris' theories, for example, is that the reason human beings are prone to monogamy is because during prehistoric life, it was important for the male hunters to be able to leave to go off on a hunt trusting that their mate would not get impregnated with another man's child while he was gone.

In 1971, Albert Mehrabian, a professor of psychology, theorized in his book Silent Messages that communication can be broken down into a three-part ratio. Mehrabian held that communication consisted of: seven percent words, 38% tone of voice, and 55% body language. This theory was based on two of his studies, namely Decoding of Inconsistent Communication and Inference of Attitudes from Non-Verbal Communication in Two Channels.

Despite the above scientists papering their theories on body language in the seventeenth, nineteenth and twentieth centuries, body language itself actually began to develop four and a half million years ago, back when Australopithecines roamed the African plains. The African continent's climate had begun to change. Where the land had previously been green and fertile, the plains were suddenly barren and tainted yellow with the windswept dried-up dust. Australopithecines was faced with the ever-growing challenge of finding food, and so, they began working in teams. Of course, teamwork requires a certain degree of communication. This newly required non-verbal communication put an incredible strain on Australopithecines' brains—a strain that led their brains to grow from approximately 500cc to approximately 800cc two and a half million years ago. Despite this incredible increase in their brain size, Australopithecines still spent about a fifth of their time grooming each other's fur in order to bond.

About a million years ago, the first Homo erectus appeared, and the forefathers of humankind as we know it today started emigrating out of Africa.

Then, 200,000 years ago, Homo sapiens evolved. They were an improvement even on the very-social Australopithecines and had a brain volume of about 1400cc. Language was developed 50,000 years ago, and everything changed after that. Human beings no longer needed to spend 20% of their time grooming each other to bond, and gossiping quickly took its place.

All human beings alive today are the descendants of the small group of Homo sapiens who lived 50,000 years ago—and thus, it is not really surprising that we all share some universal expressions as part of our body language.

Chapter 11: Common Examples Of Propaganda

Propaganda is the spread of info or ideas with the purpose of affecting emotions or actions. Propaganda is always prejudiced and can be negative or positive, but generally has a negative connotation.

Building a psychological image - A political leader will present a picture of what the world would be like with immigration or criminal offense so that the citizens will come up with that image and believe that voting for him will minimize that threat.

Overemphasizing participation - The concept of "Get on the Bandwagon" is appealing to a huge number of people by finding typical threads, like religion, race, or occupation. The theme here is "everybody else is doing it, and so should you."

Building incorrect pictures - Presidents try to seem "typical folks" but they really aren't. Examples are Bill Clinton eating at McDonald's or Ronald Reagan slicing wood.

Generating worry - Fear is created to change individuals' behavior. An ad will show a bloody accident then remind people to wear their seatbelts.

Appealing joy - Selling happiness is a concept used in advertisements, such as a favored star will explain why you need to purchase an item so as to resolve a problem.

Creating an incorrect issue - An example of false issue is where two choices are offered just as though they are the only 2 choices. For instance, a president saying in order to reduce the deficit, we have to either tax the rich more or ask senior citizens to pay more for Medicare.

Using slogans - If a motto is repeated enough times, eventually the general public will come to actually believe it.

Attracting custom - good feelings are created by the ideas of certain items and actions, and are regularly included in advertisements like: "Baseball, apple pie, and Chevrolet."

Exaggerating - By taking a quote out of setting a misconception can be given to the reader or listener. For the film Live Free or Pass Away Tough, Jack Mathews was priced estimate as saying, "Hysterically ... entertaining." The real quote is, "The action in this fast-paced, hysterically overproduced and surprisingly entertaining movie is as reasonable as a Roadway Runner cartoon."

Name calling - An example of name contacting propaganda would be: "My challenger is an alcoholic"

Assertion - This exists a fact without any proof, as in "This is the best cavity-fighting tooth paste out there."

Warfare

Propaganda is a part of war, both in the past and in existing times. Here are examples:

In 2013, Iran revealed images of their new stealth fighter flying over Mount Damavand in Northern Iran. It was quickly discovered that it was photoshopped.

Throughout the McCarthy Period, mass media tried to persuade everybody that Communists were taking over the United States.

Alexander the Great frightened an army by leaving armor and helmets that were large when they pulled back. This made them appear like giants.

In Vietnam, Americans took Vietnamese fishermen to an isle and showed them a resistance group. When they returned, the anglers told everybody and the Vietnamese spent a ton of time and effort trying to remove this fake group.

The United States dropped brochures over Iraq telling people that Saddam Hussein was responsible for their suffering.

Deliberateness and a relatively heavy emphasis on manipulation distinguish propaganda from table talk or the free and easy exchange of ideas. Propagandists have a defined goal or set of objectives. To achieve these, they intentionally select facts, arguments, and screens of symbols and present them in ways they think will have the most impact. To make the most of influence, they may omit or distort essential facts or just lie, and they may try to divert the attention of the reactors (the people they're trying to sway) from everything but their own propaganda.

150

Comparatively purposeful selectivity and control also differentiate propaganda from education. Educators try to present different sides of an issue-- the grounds for doubting as well as the grounds for believing the declarations they make, and the disadvantages and the benefits of every imaginable strategy. Education aims to induce reactors to collect and assess evidence for themselves and assists them in learning the strategies for doing so. It must be noted, though, that some propagandists may consider themselves as teachers and might really believe that they're saying the purest truth, that they are emphasizing or distorting certain elements of the truth only to make a legitimate message more persuasive, or that the courses of action that they recommend are in simple fact the best actions that the reactor could take. By the same token, the reactor who concerns the propagandist's message as self-evident truth may come up with it as academic;

this often seems to be the case with "true followers"-- dogmatic reactors to dogmatic spiritual, social, or political propaganda. "Education" for someone might be "propaganda" for another.

Propaganda And Related Concepts

Associations of the term propaganda

The word propaganda itself, as used in current centuries, apparently originates from the title and work of the Congregatio de Propaganda Fide (Parish for Propagation of the Faith), a company of Roman Catholic cardinals established in 1622 to carry on missionary work. To tons of Roman Catholics the word may for that reason have, at least in missionary or ecclesiastical terms, an extremely decent association. But even to these individuals, and definitely to many others, the term is usually a pejorative one tending to connote such things as the discredited atrocity stories and stealthily mentioned war goals of World Wars I and II, the operations of the Nazis' Ministry of Public Knowledge and Propaganda, and the broken project pledges of 1000 politicians. Moreover, it is similar to numerous circumstances of incorrect and misleading advertising (specifically in countries using Latin languages, in which propagande commerciale or some equivalent is a common term for industrial marketing).

To informed students of the history of communism, the term propaganda has yet another connotation, associated with the term agitation. The two terms were first used by the Russian philosopher of Marxism Georgy Plekhanov and later elaborated on by Vladimir Ilich Lenin in a pamphlet What Is to Be Done? (1902), in which he specified "propaganda" as the reasoned usage of historical and scientific arguments to indoctrinate the educated and enlightened (the mindful and educated publics, in the language of today's social sciences); he described "agitation" as the use of mottos, parables, and half-truths to make use of the complaints of the ignorant and the unreasonable. Since he regarded both methods as definitely important to political triumph, he integrated them in the term agitprop. Every unit of historical communist parties had an agitprop area, and to the communist the application of propaganda in Lenin's sense was good and truthful. Therefore, a standard Soviet manual for teachers of social sciences was entitled Propagandistu politekonomii (For the Propagandist of Political Economy), and a pocket-sized brochure released weekly to suggest prompt slogans and brief arguments to be used in speeches and discussions amongst the masses was called Bloknot agitatora (The Agitator's Note pad).

Indications, symbols, and media that are used in contemporary propaganda

Contemporary propagandists with money and creativity can use a really large range of indications, signs, and media to communicate their messages. Indications are simply stimuli--" info bits" capable of promoting, in some way, the human organism. These consist of noises, just like words, music, or a 21-gun salvo; gestures (a military salute, a thumbed nose); postures (a tired depression, folded arms, a sit-down, a stylish bearing); structures (a monolith, a building); items of clothes (a uniform, a civilian suit); visual indications (a poster, a flag, a picket sign, a badge, a printed page, a celebratory postage stamp, a swastika scrawled on a wall); and so on and on.

A symbol is an indication having a specific meaning for a given reactor. Two or more reactors might obviously connect rather different meanings to the exact same sign. Thus, to Nazis the swastika was a sign of racial superiority and the crushing armed force may of the German Volk; to some

Asiatic and North American tribes it is a sign of universal peace and happiness. Some Christians who think a cross is assuring might find a hammer and sickle displeasing and might derive no religious satisfaction at all from a Muslim crescent, a Hindu cow, or a Buddhist lotus.

The contemporary propagandist can employ elaborate social-scientific research facilities, unknown in previous epochs, to conduct opinion studies and psychological interviews in efforts to learn the symbolic meanings of given indications for given reactors around the globe and to discover what signs leave given reactors indifferent since, to them, these signs are without meaning.

Media are the means -- the channels-- used to communicate signs and signs to the designated reactor or reactors. A thorough stock of media used in 20th- and 21st-century propaganda could cover a lot of pages. Electronic media include email, blogs, Web- or application (app)- based social networking platforms just like Facebook and Twitter, and electronic versions of originally printed media just like papers, publications, and books. Printed media include, in addition to those just discussed, letters, handbills, posters, billboards, and handwriting on walls and streets. Amongst audiovisual media, the Web and tv might be the most powerful for lots of purposes. Both can communicate a great many types of indications all at once; they can gain heavy effect from mutually reinforcing gestures, words, postures, and sounds and a background of symbolically substantial leaders, celebrities, historical settings, architectures, flags, music, placards, maps, uniforms, insignia, cheering or jeering mobs or studio audiences, and staged assemblies of prominent or powerful people. Other audiovisual media include public speakers, motion pictures, theatrical productions, marching bands, mass demonstrations, picketing, face-to-face conversations between individuals, and "talking" shows at fairs, expositions, and art programs.

The bigger the propaganda business, the more crucial are such mass media as the Internet and tv and also the organizational media-- that is, pressure groups set up under leaders and technicians who are experienced in using a lot of sorts of signs and media to convey messages to particular reactors. Vast systems of diverse organizations can be developed in the hope of reaching leaders and fans of all groups (organized and messy) in an offered area, like a city, area, country or union of countries, or the whole world. Pressure companies are particularly necessary, for example, in carefully fought sales campaigns or political elections, specifically in socially heterogeneous areas that have incredibly divergent local customs, ethnic and linguistic backgrounds, and academic levels and extremely unequal paycheck distributions. Diversities of these sorts make it necessary for items to be marketed in local terms and for political candidates to seem good friends of every of maybe a dozen or more mutually hostile ethnic groups, of the educated and the uneducated, and of the very rich and also the poverty-stricken.

Development of the Theory of Propaganda

Early commentators and theories

The archaeological remains of ancient societys indicate that stunning clothing and palaces, excellent statues and temples, magic tokens and insignia, and intricate legal and spiritual arguments have been used for thousands of years, presumably to convince the typical people of the supposed greatness and super prowess of kings and priests. Useful legends and parables, quickly remembered proverbs and lists of rules-- just like the Ten Commandments of Judaism and

Christianity and the Hindu Manu-smriti (Laws of Manu)-- and highly selective chronicles of rulers' achievements have been used to get mass support for specific social and spiritual systems. Very most likely, much of what was said in antiquity was sincere, in the sense that the underlying religious and social assumptions were so fully accepted that the warlords' spokespersons, the pharaohs' priests, and their audiences really believed all or the majority of what was communicated and hence did not deliberate or theorize very much about alternative arguments or means of persuasion.

The organized, detached, and intentional analysis of propaganda-- in the West, at least-- may have started in Athens about five-hundred BCE, as the research study of rhetoric (Greek: "the technique of orators"). The tricks of using sonorous and solemn language, thoroughly gauged humour, artful congeniality, appropriate

160

mixtures of logical and illogical argument, and flattery of a jury or a mob were created from the actual practices of successful lawyers, demagogues, and politicians. Fairly moral teachers just like Isocrates, Plato, and Aristotle put together guidelines of rhetoric (1) to make their own arguments and those of their students more persuasive and (2) to design counterpropaganda against opponents and also (3) to teach their students how to identify the logical fallacies and sob stories of demagogues.

Early students of rhetoric also analyzed what contemporary analysts would call the issue of source credibility-- what speakers can say or do to convince their hearers that they're telling the truth, are well-intentioned, are public-spirited, etc. For example, an Athenian lawyer defending an undersized man on trial for murder might instruct him to say to a jury: "Is it likely that an undersized man like me, so often mocked for being awkward with a sword, would have attacked and killed this extremely tall war veteran who is well-known everywhere for his swordsmanship?" But a really tall and strong defendant might be told to invert the plea: "Would any man of my uncommon height, who is rather well known to have killed 300 Persians in sword fights, have permitted himself to be drawn into a quarrel with this undersized man-- understanding full well that a jury of realistic Athenians would be inclined from the start to hold me guilty if a person killed him?" So well did Greek rhetoricians evaluate the arts of legal sophistry and political demagoguery that their efforts were mimicked and further developed in Rome by such figures as Cicero and Quintilian. Aristotle's Rhetoric and similar works by others have, indeed, acted as model texts for Western experts and students from antiquity to the present day.

There have been similar lines of thought in other major civilizations. The Buddha in old India and Confucius in old China, both promoted, much as Plato had, the use of truthfulness, "good" rhetoric, and "correct" forms of speech and writing as means of encouraging people, by both precept and example, to live the good life. In the 4th century BCE in India, Kautilya, a Brahman actually believed to have been chief minister to the emperor Chandragupta, reputedly wrote the Artha-shastra (" The Science of Material Gain"), a book of advice for rulers that has typically been compared with Plato's Republic and Niccolò Machiavelli's much later work The Prince (1513). Kautilya went over, in some detail, the use of mental warfare, both overt and clandestine, in efforts to interrupt an opponent's army and catch his capital. Overtly, he said, the propagandists of a king should announce that he can do magic, that God and the best guys are on his side, and that all who support his war objectives will reap advantages. Discreetly, his representatives should infiltrate his opponents' and potential adversaries' kingdoms, spreading defeatism and deceptive news among their people, especially in capital cities, amongst leaders, and among the armed forces. In specific, a king needs to use only Brahmans, certainly the holiest and best of men, as propagandists and diplomatic arbitrators. These morally irreproachable specialists should cultivate the goodwill of their king's friends, and of friends of his good friends, and also should woo the opponents of his enemies. A king ought to not wait, though, to break any friendships or alliances that are later found to be unfavorable.

Comparable advice is found in Bingfa (The Art of War) by the Chinese theorist Sunzi, who wrote at about the same time. "All warfare," he said, "is based upon deceptiveness. Thus, when able to attack, we should appear not able; when using our forces, we should appear inactive; when we're near, we must make the adversary actually believe that we're far away; when far, we must make him actually believe we are near. Hold out baits to lure the adversary. Feign disorder, and squash him."

Spread and in some cases enlightening have a comment on political and religious propaganda has happened in all major societys. In old Greece and Rome there was much writing on election strategies. In 16th-century Italy, Machiavelli discussed, very much like Kautilya and Sunzi, making uses of calculated piety and duplicity in peace and war. In Shakespeare's plays, Mark Antony (in Julius Caesar) and the Duke of Buckingham (Richard III) show the principles of propaganda and discuss them in words and principles that anticipate 20th-century behavioral scientists. They describe such propaganda stratagems as the seizure and monopolization of propaganda efforts, the displacement of regret onto others (scapegoating), the presentation of oneself as morally exceptional, and the coordination of propaganda with violence and bribery.

Why propaganda is more harmful in the digital age

The strategies are the same, yet now anyone can go viral.

On July 6, 1916, a poster depicting Uncle Sam beckoning audiences to enlist in the USA Army appeared in a problem of Leslie's Weekly, a well-known U.S. magazine. The poster's creator, James Montgomery Flagg, had not the slightest idea just how well-known his creation would become. Working without a design or idea in a narrow window of time right before publication, Flagg scrambled to embody the seriousness of American participation in the Great War.

Regardless of the rush, Flagg created a masterpiece. It would go on to be reprinted more than 4 million times by 1918 and become a permanent part of American culture. Even though propaganda posters have been phased out in favor of more contemporary, effective means of communication, the exact same mental strategies of control that made Flagg's masterpiece so effective continue to pervade our society.

Today, propaganda posters have been replaced by digital visuals, just like the meme, that are easily produced, mass-disseminated and politically pointed, with the potential to do even greater damage to American politics and society than propaganda posters did a century ago.

Partially just because of the appeal of Flagg's Uncle Sam rendering, posters quickly ended up being a wildly popular medium for disseminating information. They were reasonably cheap to produce and could be plastered almost everywhere, from post offices to schools to sides of structures. The government used emotional imagery to draw countless volunteers to the armed services and produce broad support for the war effort in the home. Officials zeroed in on increasing spirits, motivating conservation, decreasing errors at work, promoting office safety and prompting viewers to buy United States bonds to help fund the war.

Flagg, a veteran artist and contributor to publications just like Life publication, ended up creating almost 50 designs on behalf of the Committee on Public Info, the USA propaganda and intelligence arm, by the end of World War I.

Flagg's most iconic poster depicted the figure of a gallantly dressed Uncle Sam with the popular text, "I Want You for the USA Army." Flagg found inspiration in Alfred Leete's picture of Lord Kitchener prompting Brits to join the war cause. In an effort to save cash by not hiring a model, Flagg used his own face (adding a goatee) to produce Uncle Sam, a relocation later lauded by President Franklin D. Roosevelt. While Uncle Sam dated to the War of 1812, Flagg brought it to life, giving the character an air of purpose that has itself become renowned.

The poster, formally adopted by the Army in 1917, ended up being a reliable enrollment tool to swell the ranks of the armed force. It was such a definite success that it would be reprinted during The second world war and pops up again and again in pop culture today.

These results clarify why the propaganda poster became so well-known with federal government authorities: It was tremendously effective. So reliable, in fact, that coinciding with the publication of the original Kitchener recruitment poster in September 1914, the British army saw the greatest number of volunteers enlist for the entire period of the war. In the United States, striking visuals and simple mottos drove home patriotic ideal visions and classic themes that stuck to people.

So many posters looked to yank at Americans' heartstrings with representations of warriors and their families, while others attracted the population's sense of outrage by advising audiences of the cruelty of the opponent. Some even aimed to produce a sense of guilt. In one World War I poster, a guy is playing with his children as they ask him, "Daddy, what did YOU do throughout the Great War?"

This messages showed one element of why wartime posters were so efficient: In the words of William Bird and Harry Rubenstein, propaganda posters were an "representative for making the war aims the personal objective of each person." The posters also taken advantage of the ability of psychological messages inherent in visual art to modify the subconscious. Edward Bernays, called the "dad of public relations," named his 1928 book "Propaganda," arguing that "engineering consent" through such means was crucial for the survival of democracy. The truth is, contemporary marketing owes much of its existence to visual propaganda techniques.

Posters remained a popular form of government communication in the interwar years. For instance, public wellness programs used posters to motivate exercise and preservation and promote national forests.

The appeal and effectiveness of Flagg's creation led the USA military to restore the poster format throughout World War II, when some 200,000 designs were used. These posters included such renowned characters as Rosie the Riveter saying "We Can Do It," as well as others calling citizens to arms, advising people about preservation and recycling and fomenting political and societal unity.

There was an occasional dark side to these posters too: So many uttered racist, xenophobic and bigoted messages in an effort to demonize the enemy. While this was more typical in countries such as Nazi Germany, where Hitler's brutal routine used propaganda to demonize the Jewish population, American posters were not above stereotypes and bigoted messages, at times portraying foes as barbarian brutes with racist depictions of their leaders.

Today, the poster has mostly been relegated to college dorm rooms and movie theaters. But lots of the principles that were at play in propaganda posters throughout World Wars I and II have developed as approaches of control. The digital age has introduced a brand-new form of artistic expression: the meme.

While memes initially had a comedic purpose, they got into the political realm in a far more ominous way throughout the

2016 governmental campaign. Like the propaganda posters from the world wars, politically pointed memes employed a striking visual coupled with reliable communication intended to change the mind frame or subconscious of an audience. In a lot of cases, they also aimed to dehumanize the opposition and to customize the political cause in question.

The alt-right in specific weaponized the meme format to spread disinformation through social media. Members of the alt-right turned characters such as Pepe the Frog into signs for their virulently racist movement, building awareness of and even support for their cause. The meme propaganda came from foreign sources, too, as reports of Russian bots spreading out disunity appeared.

Most worryingly, the new political art format has far greater viral potential than the posters of yesteryear. Rather than just government-commissioned posters, any figure, domestic or worldwide, with a political agenda can reach a mass audience with weaponized symbols, images and digital art to advance a political cause.

Ultimately, propaganda posters can teach us a great deal about the mental impacts of politically pointed art. While memes may appear like the silly mess of Web culture, research studies of advertising and the way we consume information have revealed that such images can modify our subconscious, often in ways we don't comprehend. Or as one Garfield meme put it, "You are not unsusceptible to propaganda." And the durability of propaganda is readily apparent-- Flagg's own creation of Uncle Sam pointing a finger at us has long outlived its original intent. In lots of ways, it has become a staple of Americana.

The threat with memes is that the visuals are no longer centrally orchestrated pieces, designed to advance the general public good. They spread in real time, seemingly from the depths of the Web, and essentially any person can attain virality through the power of mass duplication. Critical facts from fiction has become the real obstacle with this most current incarnation of visual propaganda. Time will tell if memes will become a long-term part of our political history, but for now, we're still experiencing their unforeseeable results.

Chapter 12: Gaslighting- A History Before Hollywood

Gaslighting is one of the most artful methods of dark psychology, and it requires a long-time commitment, similar to brainwashing. Gaslighting and brainwashing share other similarities, but gaslighting is quieter and less obvious. Like we touched upon in the overview, the term is from the title of a 1938 play by British author Patrick Hamilton.

In the play, which was later made into a film starring Ingrid Bergman and for which she won an Oscar, a young woman gives up her career as an opera singer to get married to a seemingly perfect and charming man. Once married, she begins to wonder where her husband is going during a series of absences and eventually is led to discover his terrible secret. As the story unfolds, we see her husband attempting to wear down her psyche by making her question her own sanity- this is portrayed visually by the gas lamps in their home dimming every time he is on one of his unexplained outings, which makes the woman feel as though she is losing her sense of reality.

The Psychology Behind Gaslighting

The human brain is wired to accept that what we can perceive with our senses is a reality. Things we can touch, see, hear, and smell- those things are right in front of us and therefore, they are real. When someone is being gaslit, they begin to question their perceptions and reality. Eventually, they accept that their new, altered perceptions **are** their new reality.

This is because gaslighting is, in general, very subtle. The changes happen over time, gradually, until the subject has no choice but to accept them. The brain becomes accustomed to the changes as they occur and eventually, the subject arrives at the conclusion that things must be all in their head and finally, their reality has become what the perpetrator wants it to be.

In the case of the characters in the play/movie, the perpetrator of the gaslighting is trying to hide a secret from his wife. Fearful of being found out, he crafts a plan to make his wife think that she is beginning to lose her mind, with the eventual goal of putting her in an institution and being rid of her.

The husband removes items from the home, brings new items in, and tells his wife she must have moved the items herself and claims the new items were stolen goods. Branding her a kleptomaniac, he demands she never leave the house, for her own good. Still wrought with grief over the death of her beloved aunt, the wife agrees she must be going crazy and complies with his wishes to stay home. The gaslighting is nearly complete.

Because the play and the film needed to have a happy ending, the husband's secret is revealed, and the wife is vindicated. However, that's not how things work in real life. In this day and age, we don't have gas lamps in our homes, and we don't always have happy endings. That being said, gaslighting can be perpetrated by anyone who has the time to play out a long psychological game, and subjects of gaslighting often don't see the signs until it is too late, or ever.

By Any Other Name...

Another term psychologists use for gaslighting is 'ambient abuse', and that name is pretty telling. Victims of gaslighting are subject to the psychological bidding of the perpetrator at all times. It's different from physical abuse, which occurs in a fit of violence, or verbal abuse which could be used in anger or in a more occasional form. Ambient abuse implies that even when the perpetrator and the subject are not in the same physical location, the perpetrator still has a psychological hold on their subject so that they are always 'surrounded' by the gaslighting.

Artwork of a Gas Streetlamp, by Eloise Williams

Gaslighting, In Practice

Gaslighting techniques must be subtle enough to go undetected, but strong enough to be effective. There are any number of ways to gaslight someone, including, but not exclusive to:

1- Trivializing or discrediting their feelings;

2- Withholding your true emotions, even when asked directly;

3- Countering their memories with an altered memory;

4- Refusing to listen to what they are saying;

5- Diverting their attention or questioning their validity;

6- Pretending or denying things that happened did not happen;

7- Changing the subject to avoid confrontation about your actions;

8- Show false compassion, do things for 'their own good'; and

9- Reframe behaviors, memories, and feelings to favor your desires and perspective.

Other gaslighting techniques could include changing things in your subject's life that are of importance, like erasing emails or messages and turning off alarms, to make them seem and feel irresponsible. You could move things in their home, remove or add items, and generally make them feel ill at ease wondering where those items are. The key to gaslighting is to keep it simple, take your time, and monitor your subject closely to see if you should back off or speed up the process to achieve your goals.

Recognizing and Avoiding Gaslighting

Gaslighting can happen in friendships, romantic relationships, and in work situations. By being vigilant and knowing what signs to look for, you can avoid being gaslit and feeling the sense of insecurity that comes with it.

At Work

In a work setting, gaslighting can occur when a co-worker or manager tries to sabotage your productivity or undermine the quality of your work. They may be jealous of your status, or maybe they are looking for a reason to fire you or demote you. There are several red flags to look for and ways to combat the gaslighting process. Here are some of the warning signs, and what you can do to counteract them:

1- The gaslighter says you didn't complete the work that was assigned to you, but you know it was never assigned. Be sure to keep detailed records of all the tasks you are supposed to complete and keep the emails or voice/text messages asking you to complete those tasks;

2- Objects or files keep getting moved and the gaslighter insists you moved them yourself. Take photographs of the objects or files that are going rogue, so that you know where they started and where they ended up;

3- If a suspected gaslighter tries to blame you for mistakes you know you didn't commit, be able to produce detailed documentation of your work to show your superiors; and

4- If you feel that you're being gaslighted, check and see if the perpetrator's behavior is against company policy and/or illegal.

With Friends and Partners

Close personal relationships are most often where gaslighting occurs, and the warning signs can be a little quieter than the red flags at work. If you suspect that your friend or romantic partner is gaslighting you, listen carefully to them. What they say and how they say it can be very telling. Some words and phrases to pay attention to are:

1- Why are you being so sensitive?

2- I don't think that's what happened.

3- Are you sure you're remembering that correctly?

4- I don't want to talk about it.

5- I'm not listening to your crazy talk.

6- I'm only acting this way because I love you.

7- You're always so angry.

8- You're always so sad.

9- Don't make things up.

10- Why can't you just admit that I'm right?

If you think that you're being gaslit by a friend or partner, take heart. You don't have to go along with their games. Be strong, stand your ground, and realize that you can't change the behavior of your gaslighter, but you can control how you react to it. Some manifestations of gaslighting are as follows:

1- Having a sense of unease which you cannot pinpoint;

2- Lying to avoid the anger or displeasure of your gaslighter;

3- Experiencing a feeling of losing your sanity;

4- Making excuses for your gaslighter's behavior to other people;

5- Feeling hopeless or powerless when you're with that person;

6- Wondering if your emotions are valid;

7- Having a difficult time making decisions or constantly second-guessing yourself; and

8- Questioning your self-worth or your value.

If you've been a subject of gaslighting, you should know that you can heal yourself by distancing yourself from your gaslighter and seeking professional help if necessary.

Chapter 13: Empath

The next thing we need to take a look at when it comes to dark psychology is the idea of an empath. The empaths will be individuals who can be deeply sensitive and will discover that they can tune in to others' energy and emotions. They can quickly deal with the feelings of those around them and turn them into their own. This can be a big challenge, sometimes, if your boundaries aren't that big because you can absorb the stress and pain of others. However, if you can carefully select the people around you and be careful with your energy, you may find that you attract those with a lot of happiness and joy. You can also absorb these positive emotions in your life.

With dark psychology, your goal is to be able to find people with more positive emotions and use them to your advantage. This doesn't have to be a bad thing. But if you want to get the control and power you want, you may find that you absorb this type of energy at the cost of harming another person. It will take some time to explore this and how it will work later.

First, we need to be able to explore a little more about what an empath is. You may have heard of this term in the past, but can you define it and use it as you should? Even the most hardcore skeptics will find it hard to deny that some people seem to be more intuitive than others' emotions and needs in our world. They just seem to pick up some of the places where others can't, and it's challenging to adapt to this without having that natural ability.

The idea of being able to experience what others are feeling is not irrational thinking. Research indicates that "emotional contagion" is possible and quite common. This emotional contagion is the idea that we can capture the feelings of others (Hatfield, 2009).

Think about it: how much does it exhaust you when you are close to someone who complains and complains about everything around you? Could you start in the best mood and quickly go down and feel almost miserable like them? Do they sometimes end the conversation feeling much better, and now do you feel unhappy? Or maybe you feel bad and approach a sparkling friend who can talk to you and help you feel much better in the process? Even if you don't consider yourself an empath, this is probably something you've heard at one point or another and illustrate the point above.

This is because our mirror neuronal system will be in place and will help us instinctively feel what another person feels when we see they are acting. Whenever we observe that someone else is completing work, the same regions in our brain will be activated that we would use to do that action. This means that our minds will react to what we see in the same way they would if we were doing that. This is why we can feel what others feel quite an ell (Marsh, 2012).

What may be even more alarming in some cases is that some people seem to have something called mirror synaesthesia. This is a process in which the tactile and visual senses for them will get confused and will be able to feel that their body is being touched, merely being able to observe someone else being touched (Medina and DePasquale, 2017).

While most of us will be able to empathize with those around us, according to Dr.

Elaine Aron, those who are considered highly sensitive will make up 15-20% of our population. These people will have a nervous system that is too sensitive and will have a higher capacity for empathy. So in many ways, the kind of people we call empaths will exist, but the way their skills show themselves may be a bit of a shock.

While it is the truth that some were born naturally sensitive, many of these empaths can gain the ability of their intuition to do this, too, thanks to some of the experiences they had as a child. For example, if a child has suffered some type of trauma, he may learn some different strategies to help him survive and adapt in ways that other children may not have.

These types of survival mechanisms, some of which may not work so well when they enter adulthood, can be used to serve them and the world when used from a more empowered type of place. As an adult, the empath will have the extraordinary situation of being able to navigate through a world that will attempt to avoid and invalidate any experience they have while continuing to attract them in hopes of learning some of the empath wisdom.

Of course, most of the time, when looking for information on an empath, you will see many positives. You will learn how to use the techniques and options that come from being an empath to help the world positively. But remember that there is also a dark and powerful underground current that can result from being an empath. And although this won't be discussed so often, it's still important to know it.

Frankly, you will find that an empath, when fully empowered, will become truly powerful when it comes to emotions, and more. They only can tune in to their power and know-how to trust their inner guidance to tap into some energy, and even some magic, which is theirs and which other people may not fully understand.

This helps them get more things they need and need out of life, and they can choose to use it in a good or dark way.

Now we need to take some time to examine five ways that empaths and other highly sensitive people can experience the world differently and possess it when they decide to do it.

The empaths will be known as emotional investigators.

One of the neat things that the empathize can do is enter a new room and read it immediately. This helps them know many things. I am also able to stay in tune with some of the tiny changes in facial expression, changes in tone of voice, or even how the other person's body language will change and will be different from what the other person is telling them.

When you discover manipulation, you quickly feel how to read body language, tone of voice, and more are essential to understand the other person. Empath can grasp these changes and retain them and their meanings, immediately and practically without even trying. This offers them the unique ability to be able to read whoever they want and makes it easier for them to achieve the desired results in the process.

The only problem here is that empath has to learn how to bring out some of these talents. As children, empath was often gas-fired and told that they were too sensitive to things. They, therefore, tried to block what is unique in them so that they could learn how to be socially acceptable.

The empathic ability to gather all the emotions in the room will be adept, and there is nothing like it. You can certainly try to take it and use it alone, but chances are you won't see the same results as someone who is naturally empathic.

The empath will naturally respond to what they feel in the room. When the energy is higher and more vibrant in a place, the empaths will handle it all, and the high vibrations will be almost spiritually orgasmic for them when they are receptive enough.

Remember that empath is more likely to risk persecution in the process if they are not careful what they are doing. But once empath learns to become more empowered, they will find it worth it. This is because they know that the other risk will mean that they have to sacrifice who they are and what they know is the truth after all.

Toxic types like empaths

Toxic types of people indeed love to use empaths to start self-destruction in that person. The good news is that if you are also an empath and are willing to devote time and effort to learn how to use it to your advantage, you will find it much easier to find other empaths and use them this way. Evil narcissists will tend to empathize because they know they will be able to find many resources, support, and energy to feed themselves. Empaths can intensify the energy around them with a lot of emotional work and skill. And narcissists can see some of the unique gifts that come from an empath and will try to gather as many resources as possible to promote their goals and needs.

Think about it this way; toxic people can use empaths as their way of shortcircuiting the path to success and helping them heal without having to do the job. They will be able to take some of the compassion that empath naturally has to get away with any toxic behavior they choose, without ever feeling responsible for it. They will take advantage of the empathic's willingness to adapt and the stamina they have to catch a bad cycle.

And all this to ensure that the narcissist and other such individuals do it to help them get the things they want. They won't worry so much about how much it can hurt and drain empathy.

However, when you become an empath, you learn that you are not responsible for someone else's behavior and can take care of yourself while also learning how to take advantage of other empaths in their lives. Since you are already an empath, you will be able to use what you know about yourself, and therefore other empaths, to work on them to get what you want.

Empaths can become emotional sponges.

Many times those who use dark psychology like to work with empaths because they can take any negativity, regret, and more on their actions and pour it on the other person. An empath will often take on all that, guilt and shame, without even really knowing why. The person who made the dead will feel better because he has been able to discharge the empath, and the empath will suffer.

As an empath, you must first make sure that you have created some healthy limits for yourself. You don't want to go through this process and then find out that someone else is taking advantage of the fact that you are an empathetic yourself. But since you already know that the empath you want to work with is an emotional sponge and you can set limits so that it doesn't bounce off you, you will be able to use it to your advantage.

Most empaths don't understand the amount of power they have

The sad thing about empaths is that they don't realize they have all this power at their disposal. They assume they are there to help other people not be there to heal themselves or that they will be able to take this power and do something even more potent in the process. While many empaths will become a finely tuned tool, they will find that they are unwilling to pursue their dreams or use this information and skills to their advantage.

For an empath to possess their power, they will thrive more when they can seek their self-validation and surround themselves with other empathetic nutrients like them. And when the empath learns that they are capable of being spiritual and scientific at the same time, they will find that there is more power than they thought. If you want to be able to use the empathy within you to get more than you want, then you need to be able to use it for your good. Learning how unique your skills are and how to find others like you to strengthen yourself and make sure you see the best results in this can make all the difference.

Many different aspects arise from being an empath. This type of person is often not understood as they should be, and they fear to do something wrong simply because others don't understand them at all. While some people will suppress this ability, those who learn more about it and truly appreciate those around them will be able to use this to their advantage in more ways than one.

Conclusion

The information that you have just read isn't meant to hurt your feelings. It's not meant to make you feel bad about yourself. This information is only to help you in your life.

Knowing our weaknesses and faults only enhance our lives. Knowing things about yourself will only help you.

And if you have read this book purely to learn how to make others do what you want them to, then you should think about karma and what's right and wrong for a bit.

Last but not least, never forget that all of us are exposed to a constant stream of manipulation in our ever day lives — whether it's through the ads on the internet or TV, by a local politician trying to win the next election or your spouse trying to convince you to what that movie together.

What makes manipulation so hard to recognize and block is not its finesse or complexity. Rather the opposite is the case. Manipulation is often so trivial and omnipresent that we simply fail to see the wood for the trees.

CPSIA information can be obtained
at www.ICGtesting.com
Printed in the USA
BVHW082248170521
607554BV00007B/1380